Model
Shipwright

1972   1997

AN ANTHOLOGY

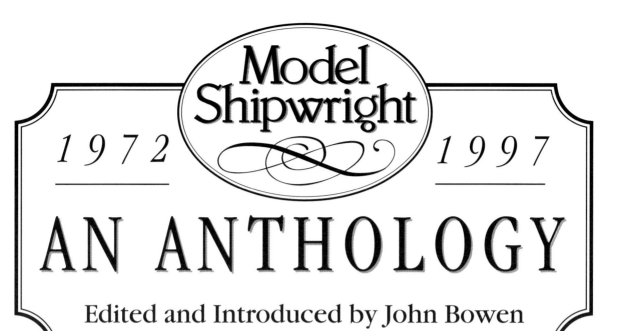

Model Shipwright

1972   1997

AN ANTHOLOGY

Edited and Introduced by John Bowen

CONWAY
MARITIME PRESS

This anthology first published in Great Britain in 1997 by
Conway Maritime Press,
an imprint of Brassey's (UK) Ltd,
33 John Street,
London WC1N 2AT

Tel: 0171 753 7777
Fax: 0171 753 7795
E-mail: brasseys@dial.pipex.com
Web: http://www.brasseys.com

All articles have previously appeared in the *Model Shipwright* journal
published quarterly by Conway Maritime Press. Year of publication is
stated in the table of contents

British Library Cataloguing in Publication Data
A record for this title is available from the British Library

ISBN 0-85177-729-5

CONTENTS

INTRODUCTION

Following a revival of interest in ships and ship models after the war, Conway Maritime Press felt that there was a need for a periodical aimed at the serious ship modeller, and so in 1972 it launched *Model Shipwright* with Arthur (Len) Tucker as Editor and myself as Deputy Editor. In those early years the journal was concerned more with the building of sailing ship scale models rather than powered ship models, though the latter were always covered. The articles have always been illustrated and accompanied, where appropriate, by plans and diagrams.

A glance through the recently-published comprehensive index will show the wide range of ships, subjects and modelling techniques that have appeared in the journal. Alongside articles on many of the better-known prototypes, there are pieces about interesting and unusual vessels such as Arab dhows, lateen riggers, Chinese junks, shallow draught naval river craft, State and Livery barges, medieval ships, lake steamers, and a number of warships of curious design. There are also many exquisite examples of the miniaturists' art, and a number of other small models.

I was thus faced with a daunting task when it came to selecting a score or so of articles from the many hundreds which have appeared over the years. Due to a limitation on space, it soon became apparent that to give even some idea of what had been covered, the multi-part articles, very regretfully, could not be included in this anthology (and my apologies to all those authors whose work comes into this category).

The past twenty-five years have seen considerable changes in the ship modelling scene, perhaps the most noticeable being the marked increase of interest in, and construction of, radio-controlled scale models of powered ships. This has been accompanied, to a lesser extent, by a similar up-surge in building radio-controlled scale models of sailing ships, ranging from square riggers to sailing barges and a number of strangely-rigged craft. Parallel to this, interest in building static scale models of all types of vessels continues to flourish. All these changes have, as far as possible, been recorded in *Model Shipwright*.

When looking at the major developments which have taken place during this time, it is worth taking a few minutes to consider them in relation to the past situation. Making ship models is nothing new – it goes back many centuries, to as far back as around 2000BC. But as that excellent book *Ship Models* by Brian Lavery and Simon Stephens illustrates, it is only from the middle of the seventeenth century that ship models began to develop the form recognised today.

But what of the forerunners in the world of ship modelling, those modellers whose work contributed so much towards inspiring others to take up the construction of ship models? A couple of names spring immediately to mind: Jason (Lt Cdr J H Craine, RN Ret'd) who in the 1930s, and again after the War, was so instrumental in encouraging ship modellers to meet and form clubs in their localities; and E W Hobbs, whose book *Model Power Boats*, published in 1929, was the acknowledged text book on the subject of the design and construction of working model ships. (Note: in this context 'Power Boats' was used to cover working ship models of all kinds, and does not refer specifically to the non-scale, non-prototype, high-speed models which today are categorised by this description.) Along with chapters on fittings, power units, transmission and propellers, Hobbs dealt with basic naval architecture, resistance and stability, and showed how to calculate the correct power required to propel a model at scale speed, with a soundly designed propeller. Unfortunately, with the more recent arrival of kits, ready-made hulls, and a good range of fittings, these essential subjects have largely been pushed into the background.

Today a modeller has access to lightweight materials and power units, and a very large volume of readily-accessible data and shipbuilders' plans. These make possible the construction of scale static models and scale working models able to operate at scale draught. Our predecessors were less well served, as the underwater part of a model's hull had to be increased in order to obtain enough displacement to accommodate the heavy power plants and batteries or accumulators then available.

Accurate plans were also more scarce for our predecessors, although there were two individuals who were working to great effect in this area.

Harold Underhill was drawing and publishing authentic and accurate sets of plans, mainly of sailing ships and particularly square riggers, from the late 1920s until the War years and for a long time thereafter. Warship modellers were well served by Norman Ough with his series of highly detailed drawings of naval vessels. Nowadays, of course, there is a very large selection of plans specially drawn for the ship modeller, quite apart from the above-mentioned collections of shipbuilders' plans.

Attention must also be drawn to the very marked increase in the standard of craftsmanship to be found in ship models of all types. This is evident not only in the larger parts of a model but also in the ability to include many of the very small fittings which do so much to enhance the authenticity and appearance of a model. Gone are the days when it was deemed that only those fittings which could be robustly made were suitable for inclusion on a working model. Now there is little difference between the quality and numbers of fittings and the amount of detail found on static or working models. The smaller models, and particularly miniatures, display a level of workmanship and detail which is amazing when compared with similar types of model of earlier times.

Before closing, I would like to add a personal note. Ever since I took over as Editor from Len Tucker in 1974 (when, regretfully, he had to relinquish the position) I would like to say how much pleasure I have derived from correspondence and contacts with ship modellers all over the world. I am most grateful for the continued help and support accorded both to the journal and to myself.

Ship modelling has made great strides in the past twenty-five years, and *Model Shipwright* is proud to have been able to record much of this progress as well as promoting interest in the construction of ship models from all periods and countries. We shall continue to build on, and to widen whenever possible, those policies on which the journal was launched, and which have led to *Model Shipwright* becoming widely regarded as the world's leading publication in this field.

John Bowen
March 1997

Ships that served

The Scottish fishery protection vessel MINNA

by P N Thomas

The first body in modern times charged with the duty of regulating the Scottish Fisheries was the Commission of the British White Herring Fishery. Their administration lasted from 1809 until 1882 when they were replaced by the Fishery Board for Scotland. The powers of the Board fell to the Secretary of State for Scotland when he assumed the Board's functions in 1939, and these were exercised through the Scottish Home Department until 1960, when responsibility for fishery matters passed to the Department of Agriculture and Fisheries for Scotland with whom it still rests.

In 1895, when responsibility for the administration of Scottish Sea Fisheries rested with the Fisheries Board for Scotland, Parliament, by the Sea Fisheries Regulations (Scotland) Act, authorised the Board *to employ such officers and vessels and to take such means*

Minna. Many of the details mentioned in the article are clearly visible in this view—the bullring at the stemhead, the 'battle honours,' inflatable life rafts, and mast details. Note, too, the radar mast and scanner and the various wireless aerials on top of the charthouse.

as are necessary for the efficient protection of the Scottish sea fisheries and for the observance of such byelaws as may from time to time be in force. From that time the Scottish Fishery Protection Vessels, or Fishery Cruisers as they are known, came into being.

The strength of the fleet has varied from time to time over the years and according to requirements. Today it stands at six vessels of various ages and classes. The most recent addition to the fleet is the *Jura* which ran trials in September 1973; she is 190'0" in length with engines of 4400 HP, and has been constructed especially for the enforcement of the outer limits and for the regulation of international agreements on fishing methods and mesh sizes, among her many other duties. The oldest vessel in the fleet is the *Vigilant*, built in 1936 and the third ship to carry this name. She is typical of the trawler-design type of vessel employed in this service; many of the earlier vessels were almost indistinguishable from large seagoing private yachts.

The Fishery Cruisers of the Department of Agriculture and Fisheries for Scotland work in conjunction with the Royal Navy's fishery protection squadron based on Port Edgar on the Forth. The cruisers may stop and board any fishing vessel within the British Exclusive fishing limits for the purpose of checking net mesh sizes and catch, to ensure that the international regulations are being observed. They also undertake a considerable number of international inspections at sea under the North East Atlantic Commission (NEAC), an aspect of their work which is becoming increasingly important in view of the widespread and growing concern of all nations in conservation. To this end, too, their enforcement of the many international, national, and local regulations and byelaws in force at varying times round the Scottish coasts, governing such matters as size of boat, size of mesh, close seasons, and so on, plays an important part. They are closely aided in this work by advice from marine scientists, the Fishermen's Associations, and other competent bodies.

The average complement of a vessel is twenty-one; these are civilian personnel recruited mainly from the merchant fishing services.

The officers hold Department of Trade and Industry Certificates of Competence, and all established personnel are—believe it or not—Civil Servants. The Fishery Cruisers lend a hand when fishing boats are in difficulties; at sea in all weathers, the vessels themselves sometimes become casualties. In recent years the *Vaila* and the *Freya* have been lost, and the *Longa* will soon be retired—reports say that she has been found guilty of making too much smoke, thus betraying her presence to offending fishermen!

THE MODEL

The *Minna,* the subject of this article, was built by Denny at Dumbarton in 1939. The first few years of her life were filled with incident. She was commissioned in April 1939 and for the following four months was engaged by the War Department in surveying the Scottish west coast for tanker anchorages. In August she was taken over by the Admiralty and allocated to the Firth of Forth for the examination service. It is interesting to recall that the first *Minna*, the present vessel being the second ship to bear this name, also served with the Royal Navy during the First World War. In June 1940 she captured an Italian steamer off May Island, and in December of the same year she was damaged by an acoustic mine which put her in a repair yard for six months. Returning to duty she was again unlucky being attacked by a Heinkel bomber in November. She was again repaired, and when she returned to service it was in another capacity, being sent in April 1942 to the Mediterranean where she carried out numerous 'cloak and dagger' operations. She took part in the Tunisian landings, and in December was credited with shooting down a German aircraft. Late in 1943 she returned to the United Kingdom for a refit, and resumed special operations in 1944, this time in the Channel and off Norway. She finished the war on a ferry service between Grimsby and Kiel. Her wartime service is recorded on a brass plaque which she wears on her forward superstructure like the battle honours of a warship. Each event is recorded, and her 'decorations' are displayed: 1939–1945 Star, Atlantic Star, Africa Star, France and Germany Star. The *Minna* is based at present in Greenock, from which port she carries out patrols on the Scottish

Top left: 'Brenda'. Built 1951 by Wm Denny, Dumbarton. 181'9" by 26'1" by 10'0" draught. 412 tons. Shown here in the overall grey livery which was standard for these cruisers until 1972.
Bottom left: 'Minna'. Built 1900 by Murdoch & Murray, Port Glasgow. 146'6" by 24'0" by 12'9". 281 tons. 11 knots. Broken up in 1939.

Minna close-up: *1 The electric anchor windlass. Note the bullring at the stemhead. 2 The foredeck, showing clearly the deck planking, mooring arrangements, mast step, and tread strips on the deck at the head of the ladder. 3 Forecastle, showing details of the ladder to the foredeck, lifebuoy stowage, and the watertight door details. 4 Boatdeck, port side forward. Note the way the mushroom ventilators are cranked through the rails from the waterway. 5 Engine room skylight, showing the steel covers stowed in racks against the funnel, the gooseneck vents (GNV) between skylight and funnel, and bucket stowage. 6 The Z boat stowage and handling davit. Note the various types of ventilators, the operating gear for the lifeboat davit (to the left of the gooseneck davit), and the runged ladder on the mainmast. 7 The afterdeck, showing clearly the construction of the hand steering wheel, the two wooden lockers, stowage of the spare anchor, and the bulwark stiffeners. The small circular fitting immediately below the stern light on the centreline at the top of the after end of the deckhouse is the receiver for the hand steering gear telegraph. 8 This view of the foremast shows clearly the foot rungs, the masthead lamps and the arrangement for hoisting the masthead oil lamp—the one on the platform is the electric lamp. 9 The 'Battle Honours' This board is fixed to the forward end of the deckhouse below the bridge. (All photographs by courtesy of the Author; these are from the series referred to at the end of the article.)*

West Coast fishing grounds.

Her registered dimensions are 175'0" by 25'0" by 11'6" with a maximum draught of 10'5", and gross tonnage of 347 tons. At a scale of 1/4" to 1'0" the dimensions of the model are 43 3/4" by 6 1/4" and at full draught she will have a displacement of about 11 lbs. The plans show her as she appeared in the middle of 1973, somewhat changed in appearance from the way she was built.

Methods of construction have been discussed in previous articles, so I will not go through them again. The main point to notice is that the *Minna* is a twin screw vessel, so it can be a bit tricky fitting the tailshafts. One method is to insert two 1/2" diameter dowels while building up the layers of the basic hull, and drill them out when the final shaping of the hull has been completed. Another way is to finish the hull and then make two templates. one to fit inside and the other to fit over the stern. Cut two holes in each, centred on the tailshafts, cut oversize holes in the hull, insert the tailshafts and fit the templates to posi-

tion the shaft tubes accurately in the hull. Then seal up the holes and form the fairing with the hull. If the hull is of fibreglass use a paste made up of chalk mixed in resin.

There are a number of details on *Minna* which I must point out as some of them are unusual and others represent modifications carried out since she was built. Right in the bows is the bullring, a heavy casting standing upright on a shaped base. The chain stoppers consist of two short lengths of small-size chain one end of each being shackled to the baseplate of the anchor windlass, and each free and being fitted with a claw which can be slipped over the anchor chain. Forward of the mast there is a steel plate on the deck covering the wartime gun mounting.

The foremast is fitted with steps similar to those seen on telegraph poles. Below the extended foredeck is the escape hatch, a cylindrical shell leading up through the forecastle. The companionway is used to form the support for the ladder to the foredeck. The charthouse originally had doors to each of

Top right: 'Vigilant' (III). Photographed off Greenock in June 1973. Built in 1936 by Wm Denny, Dumbarton. An example of the trawler type vessel 135'0" by 23'0" by 11'6". 206 tons.
Bottom right: 'Minna'. Looking very smart as she passes Greenock outward bound on another patrol.

the three compartments, but the two aftermost doors have been blocked off, as has as the second window on the starboard side of the house. Note the way the mushroom ventilators in the vicinity of the charthouse are angled in from the waterway through the rail to the inside. The dinghy was originally on the starboard side but has since been moved aft and to the port side, replacing a lifeboat. There are now two self-inflating liferafts on each side, with a rolled up rope ladder stowed between each pair; the guard rails have been offset to make room for the liferafts. One of the original davits has been left in place while the other one has been moved to the after end of the boatdeck on the port side. The deck at this point has been extended to support a platform to take the inflatable dinghy, or Z boat. This platform is of chequer plate and stands 2" above the boatdeck. There is a grating on the starboard side and on this are stowed rubbing fenders made of woven cane. The engine room skylight has lugs at each light to which steel protective covers can be fixed; when not in use these steel covers are stowed in racks on the after side of the funnel. Another addition is the wooden ladder from the afterdeck up to the boatdeck. Previously a Jacob's ladder on either side was the means of access to the boatdeck. The rigging on the port side of the mainmast had to be altered when the extension was made to the boatdeck and it looks a bit strange. The ladder on the mainmast is of the conventional runged type. The *Minna* is fitted with a large number of tanks and lockers, and all these are of steel except for two on the afterdeck. Here also, on the after end of the superstructure, is the steering telegraph receiver for the hand steering position. Stowed immediately below to port is the spare anchor. Note that all the doors leading on to the maindeck are watertight with wedging clip type handles, and a sill about 1'6" high. When built the alleyways were open all round the hull, but they have since been enclosed and fitted with watertight doors at each end.

COLOUR SCHEME

Hull: Black, with green boot topping.
Superstructure, inside bulwarks, masts, fairleads, ventilators, davits, windlass, whaleback, funnel, chequer plate below Z boat: all these are 'Fishery Cruiser Blue' which approximates to Duck Egg 16 C 33 in the British Standards Shade Card Number BS 4800.
Bridge: Varnished oak.
Capstan: Black with gold whelps.
Bollards: Black.
Boats: Starboard plastic boat light grey, British Standards 00 A 05. Dinghy on port side varnished mahogany. Boat covers green.
Waterways (gutters): Black.
Ladder aft: Varnished mahogany.
Bridge telegraph, voice pipes, metalwork on bridge: Cinnamon, British Standards 06 D 43.
(Note: Until 1972 the Fishery Protection Cruisers were painted light grey overall.)

BIBLIOGRAPHY

The Fishery Protection Service has always been self-effacing and little has been written about its work. There are many references in Parliamentary Reports regarding debates on poaching and illegal fishing, but little has appeared in books or the press.
Shipping Wonders of the World, Volume 2, pages 1433-1436: basically about the naval side of fishery protection patrols.
Scots Magazine, January 1966, pages 328-337: reminiscences of a former captain of a Fishery Cruiser. Makes very interesting reading.
The Motor Ship, January 1936: profile and deck plans of VIGILANT (III)
Acknowledgements. Above all to the staff of the Ministry of Agriculture and Fisheries in Scotland for their great help, co-operation and patience during the preparation of this article, and to the men of the cruisers themselves who have been so helpful and hospitable. To J Pottinger of Greenock for the photograph of the 'Brenda', and the Wotherspoon Collection, Mitchell Library, Corporation of Glasgow for permission to copy the photograph of 'Minna (I)'.
All other photographs from the Author's collection.

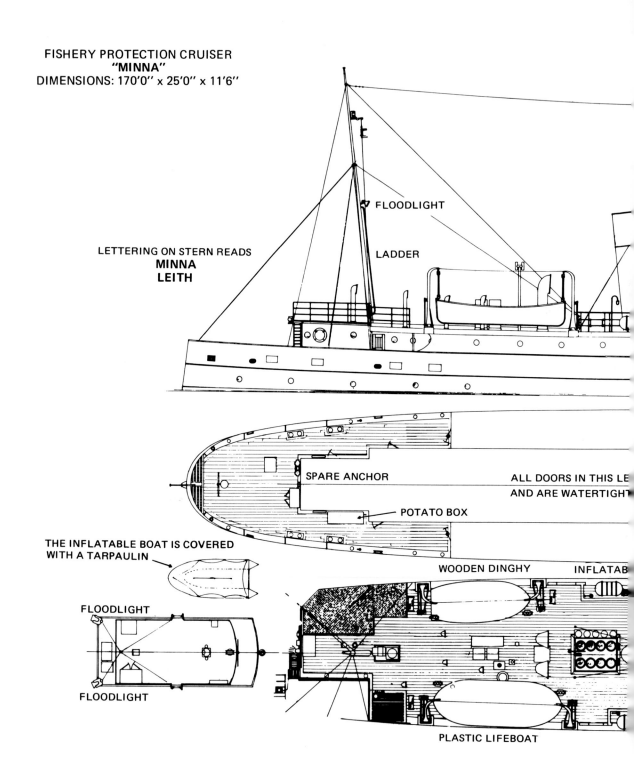

FISHERY PROTECTION CRUISER
"MINNA"
DIMENSIONS: 170'0" x 25'0" x 11'6"

FLOODLIGHT

LETTERING ON STERN READS
MINNA
LEITH

LADDER

SPARE ANCHOR

ALL DOORS IN THIS LE
AND ARE WATERTIGHT

POTATO BOX

THE INFLATABLE BOAT IS COVERED
WITH A TARPAULIN

WOODEN DINGHY   INFLATAB

FLOODLIGHT

FLOODLIGHT

PLASTIC LIFEBOAT

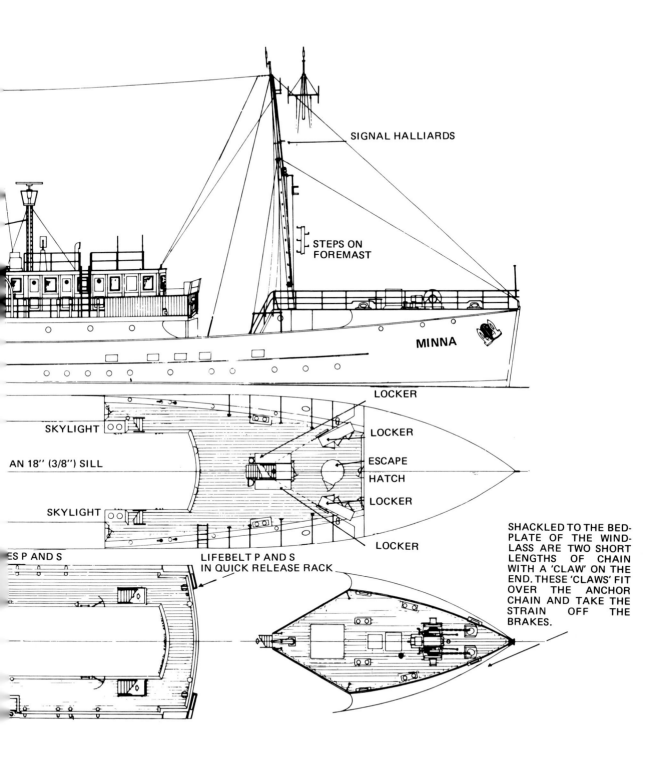

SIGNAL HALLIARDS

STEPS ON
FOREMAST

MINNA

LOCKER

SKYLIGHT

LOCKER

AN 18″ (3/8″) SILL

ESCAPE
HATCH

LOCKER

SKYLIGHT

LOCKER

ES P AND S

LIFEBELT P AND S
IN QUICK RELEASE RACK

SHACKLED TO THE BED-
PLATE OF THE WIND-
LASS ARE TWO SHORT
LENGTHS OF CHAIN
WITH A 'CLAW' ON THE
END. THESE 'CLAWS' FIT
OVER THE ANCHOR
CHAIN AND TAKE THE
STRAIN OFF THE
BRAKES.

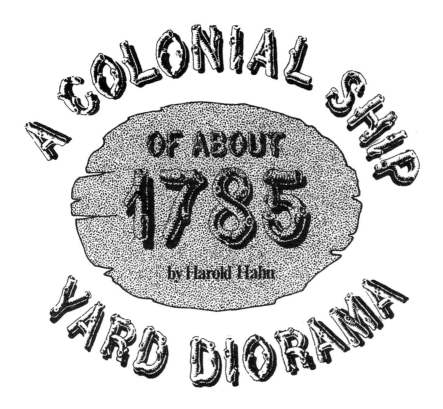

A COLONIAL SHIP
OF ABOUT 1785
by Harold Hahn
YARD DIORAMA

Some eight years ago while busy with a model of the United States frigate *Essex,* I began casting about in my mind for a new project to plan for the future. Since the 1930s when I built my first model, I had been attracted to the Colonial schooner plans I found in Howard I Chapelle's book *The History of American Sailing Ships.* One of those schooners, *Sultana,* had later been popularized in the form of working plans and model kits. However, building a model in carved hull form of a little schooner seemed like too much of a 'come-down' to follow the work involved in producing a frigate model. As a result, my immediate decision was to build a model of *Half Moon.* Still, the feeling for wanting to do a schooner persisted.

Finally, the idea began to evolve that I could justify the project to myself if I were to build several schooner models and place them in a diorama type setting. The obvious choices for this work were the plans for *Chaleur, Halifax,* and *Sultana* which formed the basis for Chapelle's chapter on Colonial Schooners. Then I found plans for *Sir Edward Hawke* in the book *Search for Speed Under Sail.* These I eventually recognised as a further reconstruction of the schooner *Marble Head* which had appeared in the earlier book. Finally, I added the fishing schooner plan which was presented in V R Grimwood's book *American Ship Models.* This gave me a variety of five quite different plans which were contemporary to each other.

The next step in the evolution of the diorama was the decision that five completed and fully rigged models might not make an interesting scene. This led to the thought of using some of the plans to produce models of partially completed vessels in a shipyard. This brought me full circle to the project which was started in

December 1969 and lasted for four and one half years.

I decided on a scale of 1/8" per foot as the one with which I could work comfortably without exceeding reasonable overall limits for the size of the diorama. Since I had carved figures to that scale before, I knew I could manage that part of the work easily. However, I had never built a complete plank-on-frame model. At first, it seemed like an almost impossible task because of the small size of the models. *Sultana*, the smallest of them, is just a little longer than 6" on deck. The conventional methods for building plank-on-frame models just did not look practical for doing the job to which I had committed myself. As a result, I had to develop my own methods for the work which provided material for articles which have been published in the *Nautical Research Journal* and *Model Shipwright*. The diorama, like all my other model work, was started strictly as a labour of love and so continued for several years. However, as my articles on related subjects appeared and were well received the thought of expanding the work into book form was suggested to me and became more and more appealing. In order to produce a worthwhile book, I decided that a serious investigation into the historical background of the schooners would have to be made. Hopefully, this would give the book more significance to fellow model builders than just another 'how-to-do-it' effort. In the past year, I have been very fortunate in obtaining a wealth of well-documented information for this purpose. The story behind the schooners has become almost as fascinating to me as the modelwork itself. *Chaleur* was the first schooner commissioned in the Royal Navy. When the Treaty of Paris was signed in 1763 to end the Seven Years War, of which the French and Indian War in North America had been a small part, England found herself with greatly expanded territorial possessions in the New World. What this meant to the Royal Navy was the responsibility for policing many hundreds of miles of shoreline which had been added by the acquisition of Canada, Nova Scotia, Cape Breton, and East and West Florida. Governor Murray at Quebec wrote a letter dated 27 September 1763 to the Earl of Egmont, a member of the Admiralty Board. He advised that the Navy ships stationed in the area were not capable of handling the suppression of smuggling of French merchandise which was by-passing the customs houses. He recommended that shallow draft vessels which could be used to follow the smugglers closer in-shore were needed. He also felt that those vessels should be manned by officers and crew of the Royal Navy.

In December 1763, the Admiralty Board instructed Rear Admiral Lord Colville at Halifax, Nova Scotia 'to cause Six Marblehead Schooners or Sloops to be purchased for His Majesty upon the best and Cheapest Terms that may be'. They gave Lord Colville who was 'Commander in Chief of His Majesty's Ships and Vessells in North America' complete orders regarding the manning and naming of the six vessels. Six Lieutenants were sent out on HMS *Juno* to serve as commanders of the purchased schooners. Colville was instructed to use the following names which would be added to the Admiralty List: *Chaleur*, *Gaspee*, *Magdalen*, *Hope*, *St John*, and *St Lawrence*. The schooners were to be manned by the commanding Lieutenant, a Master's Mate, a Midshipman, a Boatswain's Mate, a Gunner's Mate, a Carpenter's Mate, a Surgeon's Mate, a Clerk and Steward, a Servant to the Lieutenant, plus enough Seamen to make a total complement of thirty.

Chaleur's Muster Book shows that she 'Began Wages' 28 December 1763 and started Sea Victualling 11 June 1764 under the command of Lieutenant Thomas Laugharne. Her log book shows that she was at first stationed in Canadian waters but soon expanded her patrols to include ports as far south as Charleston, South Carolina. The Admiralty draught of *Chaleur* shows her to have been a tubby looking vessel. She had been built in Nova Scotia not more than a year or two before being purchased for the Royal Navy. For

most of her career she was referred to as a sloop.

Finally, the 1 July 1768 log book entry records the following: 'Carpenters employed converting the Sloop into a Schooner per order of Commodore Hood'. During this process a survey showed her treenails and bottom planking to be badly worm eaten and rotten. Makeshift repairs were carried out so that she could sail for England carrying as passengers nine soldiers and eight invalid seamen. *Chaleur* arrived at Portsmouth on 9 September, 1768. She was subsequently sent on to Woolwich where her lines were taken off and recorded on Admiralty Draught No 4518/64 in November. The original intention had been to refit and repair *Chaleur* at Woolwich but the survey there revealed that it would be 'more for the advantage of the Service to sell, than to repair her'. Thus she was paid off and put up for sale.

Next in point of time of the five models in my diorama comes *Sir Edward Hawke*, or since the two were identical twins built at the same time, *Earl of Egmont*. These two schooners were built to order for much the same reason that the first six were purchased but for somewhat different purposes. When the Floridas were taken from Spain in 1763, England acquired territory which was not so well known to her as Canada had been. The coastline which included the Florida peninsula and continued on over to the mouth of the Mississippi River had never been properly surveyed and charted for navigation. The Admiralty hired a man named George Gauld to make such a survey. The Navy commander based in Jamaica was instructed to give Mr Gauld whatever assistance he required. Once again it became evident that the Navy lacked the shallow draft vessels needed for the task at hand.

Admiral Parry in command at Jamaica made the request to the Admiralty. The result was that Captain Arthur Kennedy of the *Coventry*, 28, based at New York received instructions to have two schooners built at that city which were to be put under Admiral Parry's command

as soon as possible. The two new schooners were built with the greatest expedition until it became time to furnish them with masts which were for some reason hard to obtain. It was also difficult to man the schooners for delivery to Jamaica with qualified seamen so that Kennedy had to use some from his own crew leaving *Coventry* short handed. Because of these difficulties the two new vessels did not arrive in Jamaica until September of 1767 and did not become active in the service for which they were intended until November of that year. When he commissioned them, Admiral Parry took the liberty of naming one for Sir Edward Hawke who was First Lord of the Admiralty at the time and the other one for the Earl of Egmont who was also a member of the Admiralty Board. Records of the Board show that this naming of the schooners was duly recognised and approved.

From New York, Captain Kennedy sent dispatches which included a simple draught of the schooner's lines. This drawing No 4520/64, has as its only identification the phrase 'Marblehead Schooner Built at New York in July 1767'. The plan did not show a stern elevation, deck plans or sparring information so that the plans for a model were of necessity largely a reconstruction. What the drawing did show was very sharp lines at the bow which contrast strongly with the 'apple-cheeked' lines of the other schooners in my diorama.

The schooner named for Sir Edward Hawke was earmarked for the survey of the Florida coastline and spent most of her active career in that general area or at Jamaica. The *Earl of Egmont* on the other hand was used to 'show the flag' throughout the islands and most particularly on the coast of British Honduras where the inhabitants were described as a 'set of turbulent fellows, and who are in a state of anarchy and confusion in the absence of a man of war'. Other points of friction had to do with the French and Spanish in the area who are naturally touchy about their losses in the recent war. *Sir Edward*

Above: The fishing schooner taking on stores at a wharf.

Middle Top: The *Sultana* being fitted out, surrounded by her masts, spars, guns and anchor.

Middle Bottom: The three schooners under construction; *Halifax* is almost finished (right), the *Chaleur* is in frame (centre), and a third vessel is in the early stages of building, with the keel, stem, sternpost and midships frames set up. The realism of this scene is outstanding and compares well with Lunenburg during the building of the 'Rose' replica (see *Model Shipwright* 8, pages 427 to 432).

Opposite: The *Sultana* out of her setting. All of these schooners make fine exhibition models on their own and without the overall support of the diorama.

Hawke and *Earl of Egmont* were twins not only in design but also in length of service. They were ordered to sail for England in 1772, arriving at Portsmouth in September. The two schooners were paid off and held at the Portsmouth Dockyard. A survey produced an estimate dated 26 July 1773, that it would cost £200 to repair each of them. It was suggested to the Navy Board that the schooners should be sold out of the service and this was done on Wednesday, 11 August 1773.

In February 1768 a Sir Thomas Hesketh drew the attention of the Navy Board to 'a North American Schooner of sixty five tons which he thinks exceedingly well adapted for the Service of Cruising against the Smugglers'. After *Sultana* arrived at Deptford, it was determined that she was suitable for the proposed service and the Board ordered on 8 March 1768 that she should be purchased. On 4 May instructions were given that she should be 'registered on the List of the Royal Navy by the name of *Sultana*'. *Sultana* was quite small with a length on the range of the deck of only 50'6". Because of this she was allowed a complement of only 25 men, and eight swivel guns with no carriage guns indicated. While still at Deptford at Mr Randall's dock, *Sultana*'s lines were taken off and recorded on Admiralty Draughts Nos 4521/64 and 4522/64 which were dated 21 June 1768. Command of *Sultana* was given to Lieutenant John Inglis in July and David Bruce joined as Master. They finally sailed for North America in late August arriving at Halifax 24 October. Her log book reveals a very active career in which she cruised between Halifax at the north and Hampton Roads in the south on the lookout for smugglers. In October 1772 she sailed to England arriving at the Portsmouth dockyard 7 December. The ship's company was paid off on 8 December. In 1773 it was decided that *Sultana* should be sold out of the service. Thus it was that she was sold on 11 August, 1773, along with *Sir Edward Hawk* and *Earl of Egmont*.

In the late summer of 1768, Commodore Samuel Hood, commanding the North Atlantic Naval forces at Halifax, found that his ships were tied up on various duties along the coast. As we have seen, *Chaleur* had been sent to England in August in such condition that her return was doubtful. Needing to send dispatches to England and to augment his fleet if not simply to replace *Chaleur*, Hood rented an unemployed schooner named *Halifax* at £30 a month. *Halifax* sailed for England in August 1768 with Hood's dispatches. The schooner's owners actually had wanted to sell her. *Halifax* sailed with the understanding that on arrival in England she would be surveyed to determine if she was suitable to be purchased for Navy service. If found acceptable, her price was to be £550 and the accrued rental fees would be waived.

Following a survey made at Portsmouth Dockyard in September, 1768, Admiralty draught No 4594/64 was made and the Dockyard Officers recommended that *Halifax* be purchased for the Royal Navy. For the voyage to England, Commodore Hood had given temporary command of the schooner to Lieutenant Linzee. In his dispatches, he requested that if *Halifax* were bought into the Navy, Linzee should be named to her command. This request was honoured and after *Halifax* had been altered and refitted at Portsmouth, she sailed for Boston on 3 January. Because of disturbances in the Massachusetts colony Hood had stationed himself there in the *Romney*. *Halifax* finally arrived at Boston after a roundabout voyage on 24 March 1769. *Halifax* enjoyed the longest Navy career of any of the schooners in my diorama. From her commissioning at Portsmouth in 1768, she was active until wrecked on the rocks off the coast of Maine in February 1775. Her normal patrol area was between Boston and Halifax but she did cruise as far south as Philadelphia on occasion and made a trip back to England in the winter of 1770–71. Her checkered career included numerous changes of commanding officers, two of whom were relieved of the command to be dismissed from the service. Her duties were quite varied. Besides the usual interception of merchant vessels which were inspected for contraband in the form of smuggled goods, *Halifax* was sent on miscellaneous supply errands.

Finally, in the winter of 1774-75, Vice Admiral Graves assigned her to cruise along the New England coast in an attempt to suppress the smuggling of arms and ammunition into the Colonies which were becoming more restive as the time approached when open hostilities would begin the American Revolution that spring. On 15 February 1775, *Halifax* was wrecked off the rocky coast of Maine on the approach to Machias. She was being conned by a local pilot and it appears that her commander, Lieutenant Joseph Nunn had suspicions that it might have been an act of sabotage. The schooner was a total loss and the pilot made his escape while seeking help for the stranded seamen in company with the Master's Mate.

The fifth model in my diorama is of a fishing schooner as reconstructed by Howard Chapelle. No claim can be made for authenticity since there are no contemporary drawings to work from as with the other four schooners. However, Mr Chapelle based his reconstruction on Museum models with half models to produce the lines. He dated his reconstructed design 1785 to 1790, but it would seem reasonable that the same design could be applied to the period immediately preceeding the Revolution. This type of schooner came to be known as a 'heel tapper'. There are two explanations for the source of this name. One is that the shape of the vessel with its bulwarks around the raised quarterdeck actually resembled a shoe. The other explanation offered by the Peabody Museum at Salem, Massachusetts is that the fishermen who sailed in these schooners doubled as shoemakers in the off-season and thereby became 'heel tappers'.

Schooners such as these made up a large part of George Washington's Navy which harassed the British supply lines in 1775 and 1776 during the seige of Boston. The first of these schooners which also lays

claim to being the first armed vessel officially commissioned in the service of the United-States-to-be was *Hannah*. *Hannah* was named for the wife of her owner, Colonel John Glover, who commanded the Marblehead regiment made up principally of fishermen. Glover, himself, interestingly enough was a successful businessman who had started his career on a shoestring as a cordwainer or shoemaker. Rising to rank of Brigadier General he made many valuable contributions to the conduct of the war and is sometimes said to have given his 'awl' for his country.

While Chapelle's fishing schooner design cannot be claimed as an authentic representation of the schooner *Hannah*, artists and model builders have followed this same general pattern time after time to portray her. Since it is unlikely that anything better will materialise, we might as well accept it as the best possible reconstruction for the purpose.

After reading the foregoing brief histories of the schooners in my colonial shipyard diorama, my critics would have ample material to point out errors in my conception. In order to forestall them, I shall freely admit the anachronisms and claim immunity on the grounds of the artistic licence required to achieve my ends. The four naval schooners could never have been found in the same place. *Chaleur*, the oldest of the vessels, is shown on the stocks in a very unfinished state. *Halifax* was built before *Sir Edward Hawke*. The 1765 date is certainly questionable; I selected it arbitrarily simply as a general point of reference. As stated earlier, my primary interest as a model builder was to find a way to present the five schooners as a group in the form of a diorama. The first consideration was how to display each model to the best advantage. *Chaleur* was easily the largest of the vessels so I decided to place her in the corner of the diorama base as an unfinished hull in the shipyard. Thus her greater length would not result in an awkward arrangement or allow her to dominate the scene. The lovely design of *Halifax* made it a natural for an almost

Sir Edward Hawke, a purpose built naval vessel with the topsail schooner rig favoured by the Royal Navy in the latter part of the eighteenth century.

Top: *Sir Edward Hawke* showing the method of fitting the models into the diorama. On the right is one of the temporary bases. **Bottom:** Model shipwrights at work sawing timber for the schooner being built in the background.

completed hull on the stocks. With a third hull at an early stage of construction in the foreground, the shipyard scene could be developed to show the various steps in constructing a schooner.

Sultana was the smallest of the schooners, so I placed her in the foreground of the diorama partially rigged to show the stage of construction following the launch. The fishing schooner unloading at the wharf is representative of the typical fore-and-aft schooner rig. *Sir Edward Hawke* at anchor displays on the other hand the type of rig used on a naval schooner. I felt that this arrangement of the models satisfied my purposes in constructing the diorama.

The scene portrayed has no basis in fact and is not intended to represent any particular locale. In fact, I deliberately omitted painting the names on the schooner transoms so that they might be considered as generalized types likely to be found in such a setting. My primary concern therefore, in addition to displaying the five models was an attempt to recreate the atmosphere of an actual colonial scene limited though it might be by my knowledge of and feeling for the subject.

The background painting and the painted surfaces in the foreground were done with acrylic paint. The decision to use this paint medium was made because of the method used to produce a three dimensional effect of water. A 1/4″ thick sheet of 'Acrylite' was used in the area representing the water surface. Wavelets were produced on the flat plastic with an egg-shaped steel burr mounted in a small hand grinder. A random pattern was followed but with some attempt to coordinate it into gentle waves. The sheet of plastic was shaped and fitted into the wood base of the diorama in such a way that it would be locked in place and actually screwed down along the back edge. Before fastening it permanently in place, the wood surface underneath was painted an earth colour.

Acrylic paint was used on the surface of the water in the form of a watercolour wash. As the wash approached the foreground of the diorama it was thinned out

with a matt varnish medium and water to give it greater transparency which allowed the earth colour on the wood below to show through the translucent plastic. The surface at the back was painted with an opaque coat which blended with the background painting and with the transparent wash.

The wood base was built up on a sheet of 3/4″ thick plywood with pieces of pine glued and nailed in place. This assembly was carved to produce the underwater surface, a waterline, and finally the land area. Before the raised land area was glued in place, the positions of the three hulls in the shipyard were established. Removable blocks which would serve as bases for the models were fitted into place and the whole surface blended together. The external case was built of black walnut and to give the raised edges of the diorama surface a nice finish, strips of walnut were glued on and shaped to the land contours along with the pine. Surrounding this basic assembly, mouldings of walnut with a groove to take plexiglass sheets were glued and nailed on to form a base for the protective case. The back of the case was built on with provisions to hold the sheet of 1/4″ masonite on which the background was painted, to allow for electrical wiring, and to form a solid foundation for mounting the top structure.

The top of the case was built like a deep picture frame. The opening was designed to take a sheet of plastic 'egg-crate' type of 1/2″ deep louvre. On top of this a thin sheet of white translucent plastic was placed to isolate the diorama from the lighting compartment. Two three foot fluorescent lights were used to light the diorama mounted along the inside front and back sides of the top frame. Two slender turnings, grooved for the plexiglass windows were fitted into the front corners. A sheet of 1/4″ plywood which slid into grooves to cover the lighting compartment finished off the case.

The first order of business had been the construction of the schooner models which was followed by construction of the case and then the painting of the background scene. With the plastic water surface permanently fixed in place and painted, holes were cut and fitted to receive the hulls of *Sir Edward Hawke, Sultana,* the fishing schooner, and the two small boats. Holes were drilled to take pilings for the wharf which were pegged into the wood surface below, and the platform was built onto those posts. Brass pins 3/32″ in diameter were cemented into the forward end of the keels of the three schooners. Pedestal mounts were turned up, glued and nailed in place to receive the pins and locate the models. At the same time, individual bases for each model were made up in the same manner to hold the hulls securely while they were being rigged and to provide a temporary means for storing the finished models until they could be permanently installed in the diorama base.

The three models for the shipyard area were set up on stocks on the individual removable blocks previously prepared for them. The hulls are so close together in the finished scene that it would have been very difficult if not impossible to construct the details directly on the diorama base. Setting up the models on their separate mountings provided ready access to the work, and it was easy to set the blocks in place from time to time so as to check the progress.

The ground surface of the diorama was textured with the Acrylic Modelling Paste which is part of the paint system used by artists. The paste can be mixed with colour to suit the purpose. It dries with a flat finish which was ideal for the usage since a shiny paint finish would have been unsuitable. The surfaces of the three blocks on which the shipyard hulls were mounted were painted in this manner

This fishing schooner is the only vessel in the dioram that does not represent a specific ship, and the only one not to see naval service. (All photographs by courtesy of the Author)

before being permanently installed in the diorama base. Finally the blocks were glued in place and the joints textured and painted over to blend with the surrounding areas.

In order to give a scene like this a realistic quality, it is necessary to introduce a profusion of details placed at random. One or two of an item such as a sawhorse, a bucket, or a barrel will not even give a token effect. When hatch gratings, gun carriages, belaying pins, deadeyes and other items were made for the models themselves, extra parts were made to be placed wherever might be appropriate in the scene. Forty or fifty barrels of various sizes and conditions were made. When they had been distributed, they hardly gave the impression of any quantity at all. Several dozen tree stumps were carved out of boxwood, painted and pegged into the ground. Several dozen tools, adzes, hatchets, axes and hammers were made. Some were shown in actual use, some just scattered about. Many logs were carved out of boxwood and set aside to season until the man with broad axe could get to them. Stacks of lumber, cut off scraps and wood chips were included. Without all these details and many more, the scene would have been barren and unnatural. Even so, much more could have been added. It was hard to know just when to stop.

The trees, shrubs, and vines were an interesting project in themselves. The trunks, branches, and twigs were made of copper wire. A sizeable tree was made of sixty to seventy strands of wire twisted together into a trunk which was subdivided into large branches which were in turn divided into smaller branches until just the ends of the individual wires were left. At the foot of the trunk a central core of wires was twisted into a peg surrounded by groups twisted together and trimmed off to represent the spreading roots. All the twisted together sections of wire were heated until solder would flow to bind the wires and fill the surface which was then filed as necessary to give the desired effect. The foliage was made from a synthetic sponge material. While sponge

was not the most realistic of materials, the small scale seemed to preclude any other approach. The sponge selected as having the most suitable texture was light green in colour. Pieces were torn rather than cut from the sponge to give a natural irregular character to them. A dilute solution of dark green acrylic paint and matt varnish was prepared. The bits of sponge were dipped in this solution, squeezed out and allowed to dry. Interesting variations in colour were found possible by squeezing out enough of the paint to let the lighter green base colour show through. The wire assemblies were painted to suit and the pieces of foliage applied by putting globs of epoxy glue on the individual wire ends and pushing them into the bits of sponge.

To my mind the features that really bring the diorama to life are the many carved figures. There are approximately one hundred of them including two horses, two oxen and two dogs. Personally, I am completely sold on using figures on my models. On the other hand, there are some authorities who decry this practice. I am forced to agree with their criticism as it relates to the way in which poorly done figures detract from the aspect of a well-done model. However, if a figure is done in good proportions with a natural life-like quality so that it appears to belong, then I can find no fault with its use. Certainly, I would never have essayed my Colonial Shipyard Diorama if I could not have furnished it with a most important ingredient, people.

MEDIÆVAL SHIPS

THE 'NYVAIG' OF ISLAY 1156 AD
by J Andrew

After reading some time ago the very absorbing article on Celtic Ships ('Ships of the Celtic World', by Philip Banbury, *Model Shipwright,* Volume I No 1, page 35) I felt that some notes on the model which I have recently completed of a 'Nyvaig' ship might be of interest, since this ship is very similar to the ones described as being used by the Venetii. This is a much later version of these vessels, but the resemblance and size are very similar, since it appears that the Celts had been building ships like this for centuries.

I first found out about these ships after reading *The House of Islay* by Captain Graham Donald of Port Charlotte, Islay, the island's historian. Then on a visit to the island he showed me the Seal of Islay dated 1156, which carries an impression of one of these ships, and told me the story of Somerled, a twelfth century leader of the Celts in Argyll. The result of all this was a determination to try and make a reconstruction of the Seal ship, and to build a small model of it. These ships were known by an old Gaelic name, 'Nyvaig', a word that is now obsolete meaning 'little ship'. The ruined castle of Dunnyvaig on the east coast of Islay is named after them (*Dun Nyvaig* = the fort of the little ships).

There did not seem to be much to go on at first, only the stylised ship on the Seal first known to have been used in 1175 by Reginald, son of Somerled, and now in Paisley Abbey. This shows the ship and Somerled with his three sons who won the sea battle off the west coast of Islay in 1156 against the Vikings who occupied the island.

Back in the twelfth century, in the days of Somerled, when the Vikings occupied much of the Western Isles there was a growing antagonism towards them by the Celtic people who lived on the mainland of Argyll. Their leader Somerled decided to build a fleet of ships in an attempt to retake the islands and drive them out. This he successfully accomplished with a fleet of fifty-eight ships, after a great sea battle off the west coast of Islay on the night of Epiphany, 6 January 1156. Godfred the Viking was allowed to retreat to the Isle of Man. The 'little ship' was adopted by Somerled and his three sons as their emblem and appears to this day on the Great Seal of Islay, preserved in Paisley Abbey, and also on the cross and tombstones in Saddell Abbey, where Somerled was buried. He was the founder of the Clan Donald, and the sword and ship became the twin emblems of the Clan (Air muir s air tir = On sea and on land).

These emblems also appear on many of the ancient and beautifully carved tomb stones and crosses of the chiefs and highland warriors hidden away in remote burial places and ruined church buildings scattered throughout Argyll and the Inner Islands. The stone shown in the drawing is from the Isle of Oronsay (a 45-mile trip by boat to Colonsay and a five mile walk when the tide is out). It is a MacDuffie tombstone (Mac Dubh Sith = Son of the Dark Spirit or Fairy)— they were hereditary keepers of the records — dated 1507, a member of the Clan Donald and direct descendents of Somerled. Having searched for and seen a lot more

An overhead view of the nyvaig showing the general arrangement.

ANCIENT SHIPS OF THE WESTERN ISLES

GREAT SEAL OF ISLAY

ISLE OF IONA

KILMARTIN

KILMORY

ISLE OF ORONSAY

Opposite: The St Clement's Church ship at Rodill, Isle of Harris, dated 1527. (Photograph by courtesy of A R Cross)

of these ships on stones, I began to get a better idea of the size of the ship which I was going to model. Islay, Iona, Kilmory, and Saddell Abbey in Kintyre are some of the places where these stones can be found. Most of them appear to be similar, some show fighting tops, most have stern rudders, a few are in full sail, and others have planking indicated showing oar ports for eight or nine oars a side. This gives a fair idea of the length of these ships, for they would need to be some 40'0" to 50'0" long to give room for the rowers. The ships of Somerled were said to have been fifty-eight in number and about 50'0" long.

Some highland chiefs later had over 100 ships at their command, and the design

Below: The broadside clearly shows the hull shape and clinker planking.

did not seem to have changed much since the time of Somerled, as the photograph of the ship on the tomb of Alistair Crotach, 1547, shows, though they were much longer with a vertical sternpost. The method of construction of these highland ships would not have changed either even up to the last century. Dwelly's *Gaelic Dictionary*, first published in 1901, gives all the names for parts of a boat, together with diagrams of the construction (see sketch). The Highlanders' way of life did not change much up till then, so it is unlikely that their boat building methods would have changed either.

I decided that my model of the 'Nyvaig' or 'Naibheag' ship should show all these features mentioned above, so after about

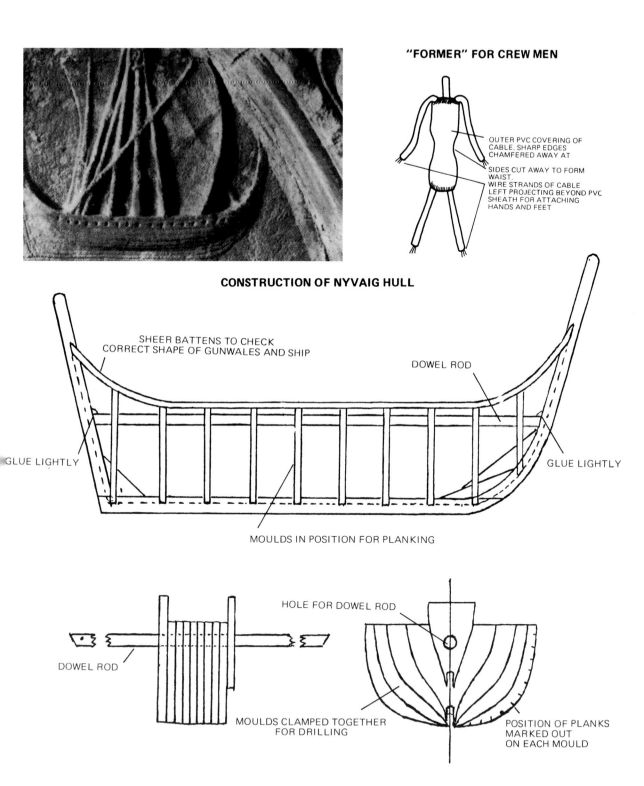

"FORMER" FOR CREW MEN

OUTER PVC COVERING OF
CABLE. SHARP EDGES
CHAMFERED AWAY AT

SIDES CUT AWAY TO FORM
WAIST.
WIRE STRANDS OF CABLE
LEFT PROJECTING BEYOND PVC
SHEATH FOR ATTACHING
HANDS AND FEET

CONSTRUCTION OF NYVAIG HULL

SHEER BATTENS TO CHECK
CORRECT SHAPE OF GUNWALES AND SHIP

DOWEL ROD

GLUE LIGHTLY

GLUE LIGHTLY

MOULDS IN POSITION FOR PLANKING

HOLE FOR DOWEL ROD

DOWEL ROD

MOULDS CLAMPED TOGETHER
FOR DRILLING

POSITION OF PLANKS
MARKED OUT
ON EACH MOULD

A three quarter stern view
highlighting the steering gear.
(Uncredited photographs by
courtesy of George A Oliver)

two years of thought, research, and a study of similar sized ships of the period, I prepared a working drawing which I considered was as near to the ships of Somerled as possible. Some of the Gaelic names in Dwelly for parts of a ship still refer to these high-prowed vessels — 'bior-dubh', the stem- and stern-posts, which translated means 'the great points'. These high prows were said to have been developed for launching ships down steep sloping beaches. 'Picteau' means shaped like a pickaxe or high prowed as a ship. 'Stiuir', the rudder, also means a tail and I often wonder if they got the idea of a hinged rudder from the action of a fish's tail.

Since these ships were about 50'0" I decided to build my model to a scale of 3/8" = 1'0", which gave me an overall length of about 20". The keel (Gaelic name 'druim'), stem and sternpost, and also the rudder were cut from 5/8" by 1/4" oak; the rest of the ship, planking, frames, floors, seats and so on was cut from obeche. The mast and yard were made from dowelling, and the sail was of stiff paper painted with red and green stripes (the Clan Donald colours). The heavy ropes for the rigging and the ladder were of thick fishing line, and the lighter ropes of fine cord. The ropes on the original ship would probably have been made from sealskin or cowhide.

I began by preparing the keel, stem- and stern-posts and fitting these together, then added the deadwood and cut in the rabbet for the planking. From the body plan I made a series of moulds, ten in all, each having a slot cut to fit over the keel. I then clamped these together, as shown in the sketch, making sure that all the centre lines were in alignment, and drilled a hole right through them all near the top to take a piece of 3/8" diameter dowel rod, making it a tight push fit. The moulds were separated and moved along the dowel rod to their correct positions, the rod being cut to length to fit between the stem- and stern-posts. Once the moulds were in the correct positions previously marked on the keel, I lightly glued the ends of the dowel rod to the

stem- and stern-posts, and ran a strip of wood round the sheer to hold the moulds in place. The next step was to mark out the positions of the strakes of planking on the edge of the moulds, and to prepare a series of templates, one for each pair of planks, and allowing 3/32" overlap. There were eleven planks each side, varying in width from 3/8" to 5/16"; they were cut from 1/16" obeche reduced in thickness by sanding to about 3/64". When I was quite satisfied with the fit, I secured each in place with impact adhesive — no other fastenings were used. Because of their exaggerated shape, I found it necessary to make the upper planks in three pieces, rather than weaken them by running across the grain. The 'nail' marks on the planks were added afterwards with a fine tipped felt pen. The moulds were now removed by cutting through the glued ends with a sharp chisel.

With the moulds and temporary sheer batten out of the way, I fitted the gunwale each side; this was cut from 1/8" square timber, steamed to shape at bow and stern. The frames were the next job, and I made these from 1/8" by 1/16" wood bent to shape and glued into position, then added the floor, of 1/16" thick wood, laying it in short lengths as in a Viking ship.

As I mentioned earlier, the mast and yard were made from dowelling. The fighting top I built up of thin tapered strips of wood glued to a top and bottom former. When all the woodwork was completed I darkened it with a coat of water and artist's lamp black to give it a weathered appearance.

The twenty-two crewmen presented a bit of a problem. It is more than likely that they would have fought stripped to the waist, bare chested and bare legged, so that if they landed in the water, or the ship sank, they would stand a fair chance of surviving. The Seal of Islay shows Somerled and his three sons bare chested, but on my model I have shown the crew in full armour, ready for fighting on land.

I had to experiment with a number of ways of making all these figures before finding one which seemed the easiest and quickest. Carving from wood I found was going to be a long and tedious job, so I tried modelling clay and plasticine. In the end I found that DAS modelling clay was the best material for the job; it is very fine and easily worked. I made the formers for the figures from lengths of three strand flat PVC electric cable, see sketch. I rolled on the clay with an 1/8″ round file to give the surface the appearance of chain mail, and used a large needle with the point well rounded off for marking in lines and so on. I shaped the head and body first and allowed these to dry, then added the arms and legs, and finally the hands and feet. Before painting the figures with Humbrol matt colours, I gave them a coat of matt varnish to harden the clay. I carved the swords and knives from wood, and fitted these to belts made from strips of adhesive tape. The spears were pieces of copper wire flattened at one end and filed to shape. I also used this modelling clay to make the sea. First I set the ship in a base cut from polystyrene foam, which in turn was glued to the base of the glass case, then added the clay, moulding it to shape to represent the sea, afterwards colouring it with Humbrol paints.

This was my first attempt at reconstructing an ancient ship, and I found it a most rewarding and interesting experience. Some of the books to which I was able to refer are:

The House of Islay, by Domhnull Gruamach; Second Edition (1967).
The Foundations of Islay, Part II, by Domhnull Gruamach (1970).
Sculpture and Monuments of Iona and West Highlands, by Drummond.
Archaeological Sketches in Scotland, (2 volumes covering Kintyre and Knapdale) by T P White.

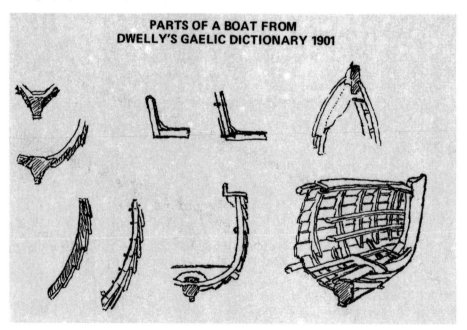

PARTS OF A BOAT FROM DWELLY'S GAELIC DICTIONARY 1901

RUSSIAN CIRCULAR IRONCLAD
NOVGOROD

by Colin Gross

Those who read my previous article on the Cigar Ship (*Model Shipwright* No 20) will know of my liking for building working models of out-of-the ordinary vessels. So it will come as no surprise to find that I was equally attracted by the description of the Russian circular ironclad *Novgorod* in John Guthrie's *Bizarre Ships of the Nineteenth Century* (Hutchinson & Co Ltd, London 1970). Before going on to describe the model, which, by the

way, as with the Cigar Ship is really an experimental model based on this ship, and cannot really be considered a true scale model, some words about the original vessel may be of interest.

Back in the 1860s, faced with the problem of defending the Russian Black Sea coasts, where the shallow waters restricted a vessel's draught to about 13′, it was only natural that the officer of the Imperial Russian Navy charged with the defence of this area, Vice Admiral Popoff,

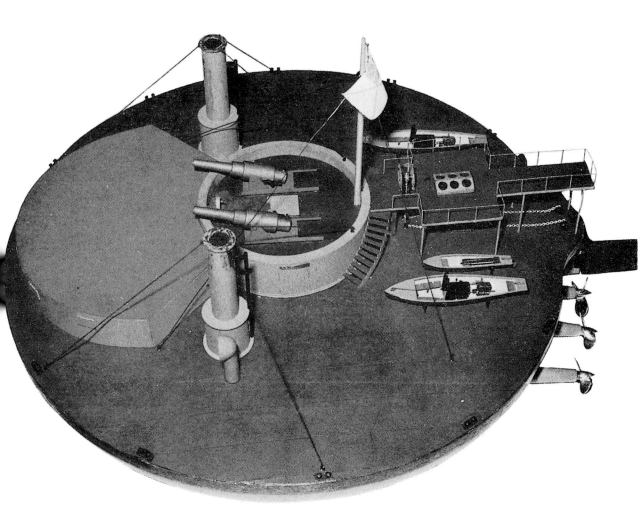

should have shown considerable interest in the design for a ship produced by the eminent Glasgow shipbuilder John Elder in 1861. Elder's idea was that a vessel circular in plan would have considerable longitudinal and transverse stability, yet be shallow draughted, and have little motion in a seaway — the prerequisites, in Vice Admiral Popoff's view, of a floating gun platform ideally suited to the peculiar requirements of his command.

So it came about that two of these circular ironclads came to be built. The first was constructed at St Petersburg in 1872, then taken to pieces and sent to the Black Sea port of Nikolaiev where it was re-erected and put into service in the following year. The *Novgorod* was 101' in diameter, with a draught of 13', free-

board of 18", and a deck camber of no less than 4'. The revolving turret carried two 8inch breech-loading guns and was almost 30' in diameter and protected by armour 9" thick. The side armour on the hull was also 9" thick, and that on the deck 2¾". The six propellers, each 10'6" in diameter gave the vessel a reported speed of six knots.

The second ship, the *Vice Admiral Popoff* was launched in 1875, and was somewhat larger, being 120' in diameter; she carried larger guns and her side armour was no less than 18" thick.

The 'Popoffkas' were unique craft, but perhaps the best known ship to be built to designs based on John Elder's concept was the Russian Imperial Yacht *Livadia,* ordered from Elder's own yard in 1880 for Czar

Below: The *Novgorod* after launching (2 June 1873). The main armament is visible amidships.
Opposite, Top: The *Novgorod* ready for launching, displaying the main features of the design and particularly the saucer shape of the hull.
Opposite Bottom: The stern of the *Novgorod.* The six propellers could not move her above about 8 knots and the outer pair contributed so little that they were soon removed.

Alexander II, to plans prepared by Vice Admiral Popoff.

The plans for the *Novgorod* were drawn up from the information contained in the above book. In plan view the hull is completely circular and in any cross section resembles a rectangle with the lower corners rounded off, a definite resemblance to a frying pan. After several lunch hour visits to the local shops had failed to provide a frying pan of the correct shape and size it was decided to manufacture the hull from glass-fibre.

Initially a large block of self generating foam, the type used to fill buoyancy areas in boats, was cast in a cardboard mould 24″ in diameter and 6″ thick. A piece of 1/8″ aluminium was then cut to a shape corresponding to 1/8″ smaller all round

than the cross-section of the hull. By rotating this around a pivot pushed into the centre of the foam a mould was produced 1/8″ smaller than the desired hull. The mould was then covered in glassfibre and resin and allowed to cure.

This rough hull was then sanded smooth, initially with a tungsten sanding disc in an electric drill, and finally with 'wet or dry' paper. The foam was then broken out from inside the hull and the top edge trimmed flat. Unfortunately the finished hull still had several 'bubble' holes in its outside surface and these were filled with 'Plastic Padding'. This operation was carried out in my lunch hour and aroused the interest of my colleagues. Within a week they had produced pictures of the *Novgorod* from such diverse sources as the *Eagle Annual* and *Playboy* Magazine. The problem was that although the pictures were basically of the same ship they differed in the position and number of cowl vents, and other detail parts. The model was thus based on the common points or in some cases the most logical position for fittings, taken from all available information.

The twelve keels were fitted under

Below: An aerial view of the author's working model.
(Historic photos: Conway Picture Library Model photos: John Bowen)

the hull, and the six propeller shafts fitted, together with their conical casings. The three shafts on each side of the vessel were connected together using 'Meccano' chain and chain wheels, each group of three being driven from the geared output of a 'Decaperm' electric motor. The rudder assembly was also fitted at this stage while access to the interior was still possible. The 1/4″ ply deck supports were then fitted together with the 1/2″ ply rings which formed the barbette. The deck was covered in 1/2″ balsa sanded to give the very large curvature which is such a feature of the deck. The whole deck and superstructure were then covered in 20 thou plasticard 'plates' to simulate the armour.

The superstructure of the model was assembled from 1/32″ ply and plasticard with brass framing where rigidity was required, as on the bridge assembly. The two 8″ breech loading guns were turned from brass, and the gun platform and entire cabin were made removable for access to the interior.

The ship's boats were made from strips of 5 thou plasticard, 50 thou wide, over plasticard frames; this simulated the planking of the hulls whilst allowing a rapid construction.

The hull was equipped with a 3 channel radio giving proportional speed control of each motor and

rudder control. Power for the drive motors was provided by two 6 volt 4 Ah accumulators and 1½lbs of ballast was required to trim the model.

The first ever trial was run at the Berrylands regatta in September 1974 and as expected the model proved almost impossible to control since the rudder had no effect on the direction in which the model moved. Despite only collecting one penalty whilst completing the steering course *Novgorod* caused several problems for the judges. On that day it became the slowest model to complete the course and the only one to do a 360 degree turn in the canal (without touching the banks), and with only 3/8″ freeboard on its 16″ diameter was almost impossible to see when on the far side of the course. Judging for 'Appearance on the water' also caused a problem. As for driving the model it was very rare to have both engines going in the same direction, yet alone the same speed!

Since that day *Novgorod* has only been used in one other competition when my only other usable model was a 6′ long 'Camship' (Catapult Armed Merchant Ship). However *Novgorod* is still kept in working order and always causes amusement and confuses the public whenever it appears, their normal comment on the model being 'Look! a Hovercraft'.

DANUBE GUNBOAT TEMES

by Friedrich Prasky

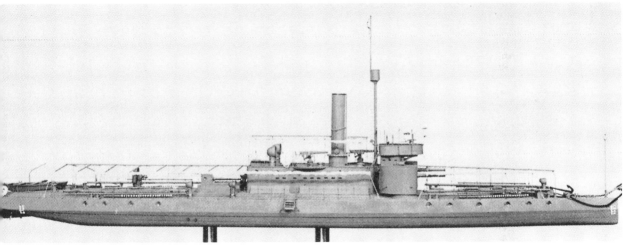

Top right: Forecastle and forward super-structure. Note the navigation lights fixed to the axis of the gun turrets.
Above: This broadside gives a clear impression of the vessel's hull shape.

The river monitor *Temes* is a rather extraordinary ship. During her life she has been the flagship of the Danube flotilla, opened the First World War with its attack on Belgrade, has been sunk, raised, rebuilt, and even survived World War II.

The *Temes* and her sister ship *Bodrog* were completed at the shipyard of H Schonichen at Budapest in November 1904. With a standard displacement of 448 metric tons, the dimensions were 57.7 metres overall, 55.6 metres between perpendiculars, 9.5 metres breadth, 1.2 metres draught. The two sets of triple expansion engines, supplied by two Yarrow boilers, developed 1400 IHP and gave the vessel a speed of 13 knots. The armament consisted of two 120 mm

guns mounted in single turrets, one 120 mm howitzer, two 37 mm and one 8 mm machine gun. Armour was 40 mm on the sides, 25 mm on the decks and 75 mm on the conning tower. The twin screws were set in tunnels, which as well as being necessitated by the shallow draught also afforded a measure of protection to the propellers on those apparently quite frequent occasions when the vessel went aground.

She was mined and sunk in October 1914, was raised and repaired in 1916, when a number of alterations were made. She survived the war and was later allocated to Roumania, being renamed *Ardeal;* she was still afloat after the end of the Second World War. Her sister ship *Bodrog* also had quite a chequered career. During the First World War she was in action against Serbia, and against Roumania. In 1918 she crossed the Black Sea and operated on the rivers in Southern Russia, later running aground and being captured by the Serbians. Later she was taken over by Yugoslavia and renamed *Sava*. In 1941 she was sunk near Belgrade, was refloated, only to be sunk again by her own crew in 1944. She was refloated again in 1945 and served as the *Sava* once more under the Yugoslav flag.

My model is built completely of brass. The hull consists of a 2 mm thick baseplate, to which the 5 mm sides were soldered. The deck is also 5 mm thick, soldered to the sides. This block was then filed to its final shape. The hull plating was etched and the side armour then bonded to the plating with adhesive. The superstructure was cut from sheet brass and soldered. Many of the small parts

for the guns, and so on were etched by a photo-chemical method. I used Humbrol paints throughout mixing up the correct shades myself and then applying them with a Badger air brush. The total time I spent on building the model amounted to some 600 hours.

Before I could start work I had to do a great deal of research collecting or viewing many documents and photographs, mostly in the Austrian War Archives in Vienna. I was also able to use the original (and correct!) shipyard plans, and handbooks for the guns. From all this information I was able to prepare the plans of which part are shown with this article.

Editor's note: We have only been able to reproduce part of the plan to which the Author refers.

Part of the exquisitely detailed plans of *Temes* produced by Ing Prasky.

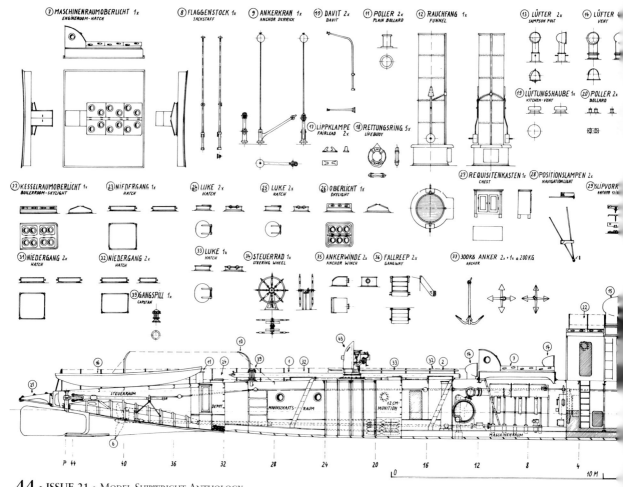

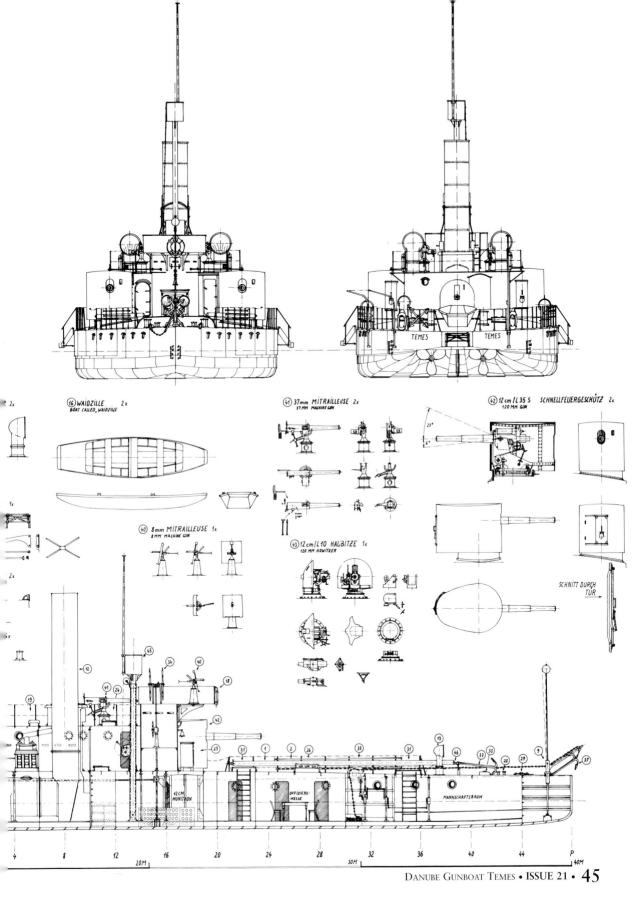

16 WAIDZILLE 2x
BOAT CALLED, WAIDZILLE

41 37mm MITRAILLEUSE 2x
37 MM MACHINE GUN

42 12 cm / L 35 S SCHNELLFEUERGESCHÜTZ 2x
120 MM GUN

8mm MITRAILLEUSE 1x
8 MM MACHINE GUN

43 12 cm / L10 HAUBITZE 1x
120 MM HOWITZER

SCHNITT DURCH
TÜR

42 CM
MUNITION

OFFIZIERS-
MESSE

MANNSCHAFTSRAUM

Right: A view forward from the quarter. Although the absence of large numbers of complicated fittings makes this an ideal 'starter's' model, what fittings there are need to be finished with skill – note the rivet detail and lowering gear on the funnel, for example.

Below: The quarterdeck of this river gunboat shows little of the clutter – bollards, fairleads, etc – associated with deep sea warships.

Opposite top: The bow, notice the flat, wedge-like hull shape and the interesting anchor handling gear.

Bottom: The bridge and forward guns. (All photographs by courtesy of the Author)

WOODEN STEAM SCOW
ALLIGATOR

This article has been compiled from notes and photographs kindly loaned by our Consultant Editor, Arthur L Tucker.

Above: A photograph from the collection in the Montreal Archives of an *Alligator* working in a log boom in 1908. It is interesting to see that there is only a wheelhouse on the engine casing, and that it carries navigation lights. The size of the anchor used is clearly visible.

The peculiar requirements of maritime connected trades and industries inevitably lead to the development of many interesting and unusual ship designs. The lumber industry in Canada and America is no exception — one has only to think of the old steam schooners of the West Coast or the present day huge, self-dumping log barges. However, it was in the vast area of shallow lakes and narrow rivers of Northern Ontario and Quebec that there appeared in 1889 a little vessel which was to become both the delight and despair of lumbermen there and later over the border in America. Known as an *Alligator* this unique craft not only hauled log booms on

the lakes and rivers, but when necessary hauled itself overland from one site to another.

In 1889 a Canadian, John C West, patented his design of an amphibian vessel for use in the shallow waters of the lumber forests. Up to that time the lumbermen had used a primitive form of floating horse-driven capstan to winch the huge log booms along these waters — 'towing on the anchor' as it was called. An anchor was dropped well ahead of the boom by a small boat, the cable attached to it was taken back to the boom, and the boom hauled or winched up to the anchor, when the whole slow, heavy and tedious process was repeated.

West's design employed much the same principle, being a steam boat carrying a steam winch. The early vessels built by his firm were propelled by a pair of simple paddle wheels, but by the turn of the century he was offering a twin screw version, in which the propellers could be raised to clear obstructions. The other major advantage of the design was the ability of the boat to transport itself overland. When built each boat had two heavy timbers or runners fitted fore and aft along the underside of the bottom. Then, the cable having been run out and attached to a suitable tree, the steam winch wound in the cable, thus pulling the vessel along; all that was needed was to have logs or skids laid across the portage trail, and it took gradients in its stride.

When hauling logs the *Alligator* dropped its anchor about a mile ahead of the boom to be moved (and

Top right: The subject of the article lying on the bank of Lake Ha! Ha! Part of the wheelhouse is lying in the foreground. The firebox end of the boiler is just discernible through the large square opening.
Centre: The bow, showing the additional sheathing on the chine and underside of the bow.
Bottom: A close up view of the remains of the port paddle wheel. Note its simple construction, and the flanged ends of the floats. The run of the radial arms can be seen, and this is also to be seen in the top photograph.

a boom could comprise anything from 30 000 to 60 000 logs), paddled back to the boom, where the paddles were disconnected, the boom made fast to the boom post on the after deck, the winch engaged, and the vessel proceeded to winch itself and the boom up to the anchor. The whole cycle of operations was then repeated.

West's *Alligators* steamed along lakes and hauled themselves over portages for over fifty years. His firm ceased building these craft in 1932, but the basic concept is still being produced in many modernised versions by the Company which took over where West left off in 1932.

CONSTRUCTION
The *Alligator's* hull was scow shaped (that is, swim ended as in a Thames lighter). The bottom was of oak planks 3 in thick, and the sides were of 6 in thick pine. Part of the bottom and the bow were covered with boiler plate. The steam engine, of 12 hp or more, was arranged to drive either the paddles or the winch. In order to keep the water in the boiler level when portaging up or down hill, the boiler was pivoted at its central point. It was fired with cordwood. The winch drum held at least a mile of 5/8 in diameter steel wire cable. Two sizes of vessel were available, 37 ft x 10 ft and 45 ft x 11 ft, the draughts being 30 in and 26 in respectively.

In 1973 an inspection was carried out by a marine surveyor of a derelict *Alligator* lying on the bank of Lake Ha! Ha! in Quebec Province, and the accompanying plan was prepared

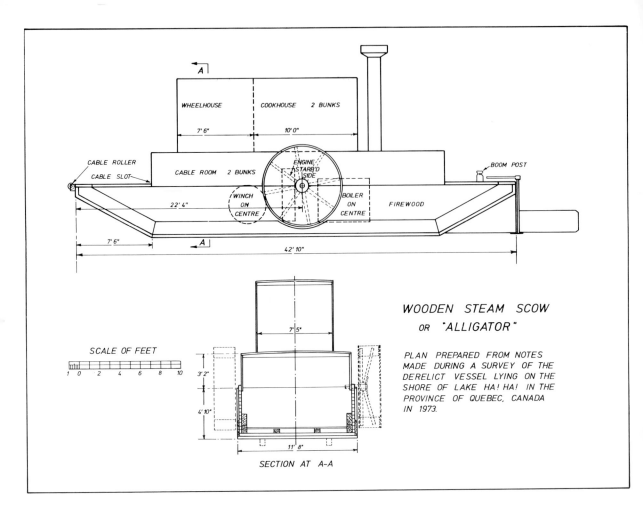

WHEELHOUSE   COOKHOUSE   2 BUNKS

7' 6"   10' 0"

CABLE ROLLER

CABLE SLOT

CABLE ROOM   2 BUNKS

ENGINE
STARB'D
SIDE

BOOM POST

WINCH
ON
CENTRE

BOILER
ON
CENTRE

FIREWOOD

22' 4"

7' 6"

42' 10"

A

A

WOODEN STEAM SCOW
OR "ALLIGATOR"

PLAN PREPARED FROM NOTES
MADE DURING A SURVEY OF THE
DERELICT VESSEL LYING ON THE
SHORE OF LAKE HA! HA! IN THE
PROVINCE OF QUEBEC, CANADA
IN 1973.

SCALE OF FEET

1 0   2   4   6   8   10

7' 5"

3' 2"

4' 10"

11' 8"

SECTION AT A-A

from notes taken at the time. This particular vessel had been assembled on the shores of the Lake about 1912 and had spent all its working life on those waters. It was laid up in 1948. As the photographs show, the hull was in poor condition by 1973, nevertheless the surveyor's notes provide some interesting further constructional details.

The bottom was of 3 in thick planks and the sides of 5½ in wide spruce 3½ in thick in laminated construction. After WWI the bow and stern and the bottom were given an extra thickness of 3 in planks, and the chines were reinforced longitudinally. The rudder was of iron, and was hung on a skeg fitted under the after part of the hull. The blade could be lifted up by a short chain attached to the after end of the tiller. Chains led port and starboard from the tiller through

sheaves on the after deck along inside the engine/boiler casing and cabin (where they were covered with canvas for safety) to the steering gypsy in the wheelhouse. In the centre of the after deck was the heavy post to which the log boom was made fast. A heavy roller was fitted across the head of the bow to carry the wire cable.

The boiler was wood fired, and of the dry-back Scotch marine type, 60 in long and 49 in diameter, with 64 2-in diameter tubes, and a firebox 33 in diameter; the boiler shell was 5/16 in thick. The working pressure would have been about 90 lb per square inch. It was fitted with twin lever type safety valves. The stack (funnel) was about 15 in diameter, and about 12 ft high above the boiler.

The engine was of the single cylinder vertical type, with slide

Top: The after deck showing the tiller and the top of the rudder post, and the sheave for the steering chain. Note that the deck planking is laid athwartships.
Centre: The rudder, with the lifting chain for the rudder blade shackled to the end of the tiller. Lying alongside the rudder is the conical top of the smoke stack.
Bottom: In the foreground is the winch barrel, still with wire on it. The large gear wheel on the right is on the paddle shaft. The steam engine is on the left of the photograph, while the various control levers can be seen behind the winch barrel.

valve and reversing gear, 7 inch bore and 7 inch stroke. The surveyor commented that the engine and boiler appeared to be older than the hull, and thought they were made in the 19th century.

The paddles were 88 in diameter, and were fitted with eight fixed steel floats bolted to wood radial arms. The floats measured 24 in x 12 in. Their ends were flanged to bolt to the steel flat bar 'rims' of the wheels.

From the control position just abaft the winch the engineer could engage and disengage the paddles as required, and by 'juggling' with a train of gears had a choice of two speeds for the winch, the barrel of which was 30 in long and 30 in diameter, and held a mile of wire cable.

On deck the engine casing was surmounted by a long deckhouse, containing the wheelhouse and abaft that the cookhouse. With a crew of six, all berthed aboard in what must have been very primitive and cramped accommodation, and bearing in mind the lonely, monotonous, and heavy nature of the work, the cook was undoubtedly the most important member of the crew!

Despite the considerable deterioration, coupled with some vandalism which the vessel had suffered, the surveyor was of the opinion that there was sufficient sound material left for the vessel to be reconstituted as an example of a unique and interesting type. As the then owners in Montreal were willing to sell it 'as is, where is' for one dollar, it would be interesting to know what happened to it.

KETCH-RIGGED SLOOP (1752)
HMS SPEEDWELL

by Dana L McCalip

One of the most interesting classes of vessel of the eighteenth century Royal Navy were the sloops-of-war. These vessels were generally two masted and rigged as snows, ketches and brigantines. They were 'maids of all work' and until replaced by heavier ship-rigged sloops in the 1760s, performed varied duties such as surveying, dispatch carrying, and escort service. They were generally lightly armed and it was rare if their main battery exceeded 6pdrs.

The *Speedwell* was one of a class of six sloops built during 1752–54

and of this class three, *Speedwell*, *Fly* and *Happy* (of almost identical dimensions), were ketch-rigged while the remainder were rigged as snows. The ketch rig, though rather picturesque, was an awkward rig to handle and manoeuverability was difficult. The rig enjoyed some popularity as a rig for bomb vessels but it too was short-lived for the same reason and bomb vessels soon adapted a three-masted or ship rig.

Speedwell's dimensions from Admiralty records are:
Length of gundeck 72.5ft

Length of keel for tonnage 60.2ft
Breadth 20.5ft
Depth in hold 8.8ft
Burden 135 tons
The records also indicate that she carried 8 carriage guns, probably 3 or 4pdrs. There are swivel stocks on the forecastle deck which would accommodate 4 small swivel guns.

The model of HM sloop *Speedwell* *c*1752 is built to a scale of 3/32in = 1ft which gives the hull a length between perpendiculars of 8in. The idea to build the model came from the desire to have a companion piece to a 3/32 scale naval cutter which was completed in the latter part of 1975 and was totally inspired by Bill Shoulder's article on the ketch-rigged sloop which appeared in *Model Shipwright* Nos 1 and 2.

MODELLING THE HULL
The hull is built on buttock lines (vertical lifts) rather than the conventional lift method. I prefer building on buttock lines as one can work with a permanently fixed centreline and the sheer can be precut into each buttock section before they are glued up. Once the sections are glued up the whole block is subsequently sawed to the half breadth. This operation will leave one with a hull block that is cut to sheer, half breadth, and due to the configuration of the buttock lifts one has a good start on bringing the hull into shape as per the body plan by the judicious use of templates.

In order to keep paint thicknesses to a minimum, an attempt was made to use hard, close-grained woods that would closely resemble the varnished

Opposite and below: two views of the completed model. Note particularly the clarity of deck detail.
(All photographs by the author)

or oiled woods used during the middle eighteenth century. I chose American cherry as it is very close-grained, is not too difficult to carve and takes a nice finish. I was somewhat concerned about it being a little too pale in colour though, and had given some thought to perhaps adding a little stain to the varnish to darken it a little. However, this proved unneccessary as when exposed to air and sunlight the cherry wood darkened in a few months to a rich golden brown. As a subtle contrast, the trim mouldings on the hull are of apple wood, which is a very deep brown. The wales are also apple wood shavings which were dyed black. They were finished by wiping on a black leather dye which colours thoroughly, allows no build-up and causes no adhesion problems when finished off the model and attached when necessary. This is a must for me as I am unable to paint a straight line and would just have a mess if I attempted to paint the wales after being affixed to the model. The deck is sap gum and laid in individual planks which scale to 8½in.

The major component parts of the head and transom are carved from apple and pear wood whilst small details such as window frames, mouldings and seat rails are made up from shavings of the same material. The scrollwork and crown on the transom are conjectured ornamentation, the components of which come from a model supply house in Paris. Any one doing period ship models with a great deal of decorative work would do well to obtain their catalogue as their

decorative fittings are most exquisitely done. Write to R Stab, 35 Rue des Petits Champs, Paris, France. The figurehead I must confess is an HO scale model railroad figure whose lower body portion was removed; details such as helmet, epaulettes and cuirass were moulded on the model with a cold water plastic resin cement. The sword being held by the figure was ground from a fragmented Wilkinson razor blade and has a brass hand guard. The sword has an overall length of ¼in and is a good

talking point, though I am not sure if Wilkinson steel was manufactured in the middle eighteenth century!

A very interesting feature of this little vessel is the glazed area on the quarterdeck bulkhead. As with most of my 3/32in models, I am able to achieve rather satisfactory results through the use of film negative which is moderately clouded. The clouded negative gives the appearance of glass and the illusion of depth even though there is nothing behind it but a matt surface. I was confronted with the problem of making the

These two views again show how essential it is to concentrate on a fine finish to the detail work.

numerous mullions that criss-crossed the glazed area. Shavings in this scale no matter how finely cut just looked too big and cumbersome, while alignment would have been a tremendous problem. I finally hit upon the idea of scratching a fine line on the emulsion side of the negative. This scratch, the width being determined by the width of the instrument being used to make the scratch, will be devoid of chemical film and only a clear strip of acetate will be in its stead. A series of these scratch lines criss-crossed on the emulsion side of a negative create very convincing mullions especially when filled with a thin coat of enamel. Once coated the excess was wiped off, taking care not to remove that which has filled the scratch. When completely dry the individual window units may be affixed in place with a touch of white glue.

FITTINGS

The hatches, bitts, and capstan were all pieced up out of apple and pear wood. The capstan was most interesting project as it became necessary to lay out the holes for the eight capstan bars at equal distances. Ideally the way to do it would be to use an indexing head in conjunction with a lathe, but not having one I was forced to lay out the positioning of the holes on a piece of paper, subsequently trying to superimpose the eight location points on to the small capstan drumhead. This method was only slightly better than trial and error as if the drill wandered even slightly the effect was terrible. After about seven attempts a pesentable one finally was turned out although there was a few thousandths variance in the hole spacing.

The deck guns, of which there are eight in number, are 4pdrs. The barrels were cast in pewter from a brass master which was turned on a Unimat lathe. The carriages are made entirely of apple wood with annealed iron wire metal work. Mounted in the bow are four 1lb swivels which again were turned on the Unimat. Due to their small size, 5/32in, they were formed with a needle file; a tool bit would have put too much strain on them. I used 1/8in stock, and prior to turning holes were bored for the muzzle and trunnions.

The 19ft yawl boat mounted forward of the mainmast was fashioned out of a piece of aspen which was a block consisting of left and right halves glued together with an acetate type of adhesive. Once carved to the outside dimensions and roughly routed out the block was soaked in a solvent which would cause the glue to let go; once apart each half can be worked upon from the inside to make it uniformly as thin as possible. When finished with the inside, the two halves are rejoined on either side of an already finished stem, stempost and keel. All that remained to do was to finish out the interior with ribs, thwarts, bottom boards, knees and stern grating. The ribs were of thin apple wood shavings which are easily cemented to the interior with a good white glue. They, like the bottom boards, thwarts and knees, need little

explanation as they can be formed up from small scraps of apple and pear wood, using swiss pattern files and fine sandpaper.

The grating in the stern of the yawl boat as well as that on the fore and after side of the mizzenmast was made of pear wood on a circular saw which was designed and built by Mr Jack Kitzerow, a ship modelling friend of mine who was also responsible for the photographs in this article. The saw is powered by a 1/5hp electric motor turning a 3in screw slotting blade which has a thickness of 0.014in. This blade, along with a special saw table with a permanently fixed guide fence, enables me to cut notched strips (racks) that are exactly 0.014in thick and with notches that are 0.014in wide with spaces 0.014in apart. The depth of the notch is determined by the setting of the table over the blade and the thick-

ness by the proximity of the blade in relation to the guide fence. The gratings are then constructed of a series of these interlocking notched strips. The notched pieces form a border or perimeter with a similar group forming all of the strips running from one direction. Those strips running at right angles to the notched strips may be just thin strips laid in the notches; however, it would be a real exercise in wood working if one used the notched strips throughout. Gratings were not built this way however.

MASTS, SPARS AND RIGGING
The masts and spars are made from pear and are turned on the Unimat using templates which are divisionally quartered based on Steel's *Tables of Masting and Rigging*. The model is depicted in her winter rig, ie rigged only up to the main topsail yard. The main topgallant has been left off and

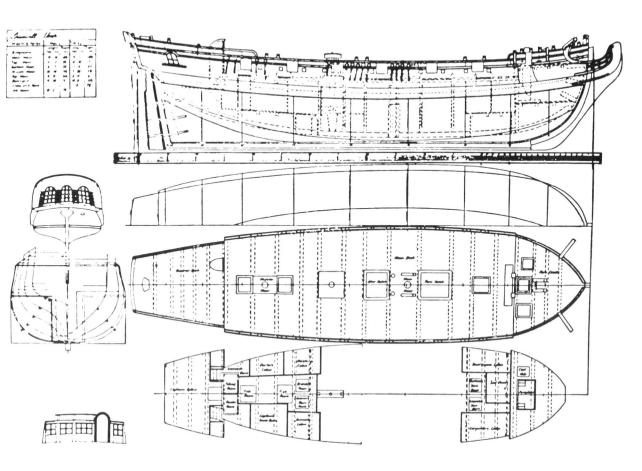

is shown as being stowed on the riding bitts and main jeer bitts with a spare main topgallant mast. This not only provided a very interesting piece of deck detail but also made a convenient place to stow the small boat.

The rigging is of linen, the smallest diameter being 0.003in. Again, Steel's book on masting and rigging was most helpful. The blocks are of boxwood ranging from 3/64in up to 1/8 in. Prior to rigging, all the cordage was soaked in a solution of beeswax and naptha. This protects the line from dampness and, being a solution, soaks the line completely with this waxy substance. This to me is preferable to drawing it through a cake of wax as this coats just the surface of the line and also leaves a residue of wax near the hole of any block or deadeye that it might be drawn through.

Speedwell is the first model that I have ever put a flag on as I have always felt that unless they appeared natural they had best be left off. I have had the good fortune in the past several years to become acquainted with some of the members of the Illinois Military Miniature Society and through the good auspices of Mr Edmund Urbanczyk was able to obtain a Red Ensign and Independent service pennant.

The flags according to Ed were made from rice paper and painted with Winsor and Newton water colours. They were then given a protective coat of acrylic spray.

This model was a most enjoyable project, and now for the most part I feel fully committed to the 3/32 scale and may try something more ambitious next time.

REFERENCES AND ACKNOWLEDGEMENTS
Science Museum, South Kensington: photographs 3866, 768/56, 509/68, 510/58, 511/68, 512/68, 513/68, 514/68
National Maritime Museum
G S Laird Clowes: *Sailing Ships* Part 2
Merritt A Edson Jr, Secretary of the Nautical Research Guild, Washington, DC
Howard I Chapelle: *History of the American Sailing Navy*

Below: note the simple and effective stern decoration and the rice paper flag.

THE VICTORIAN STEAM LAUNCH
Branksome

by D J Jacques

Branksome under way.

With my interest in steam being revived I started to look into designs and available materials. This coincided with the opening of the Windermere Steam Museum, and the steam launch *Branksome* had all the requirements for a working model. The hull was of teak construction, carvel-built and well proportioned, the length being 50ft and the beam 9ft. The boiler was enclosed and the engine had open access on the starboard side. The foredeck had a grating which would allow ventilation to the proposed burner unit. The after cabin would cover the radio and had plenty of detail.

A big advantage for any scale modeller is having the full size prototype available within a short car run. At that time no hull lines or detail drawings were available, but with the permission of Mr G Patterson (the owner of the *Branksome*) I was able to take many colour slides of all the key points necessary for preparing a set of working drawings; these included views of constructional detail and of the general arrangement.

Using a photograph showing the full side elevation of the vessel, and knowing the overall dimensions, 50ft by 9ft beam, I found that a suitable scale to accommodate the 9in x 6in diameter boiler which I had was $\frac{1}{8}$ full size. The side elevation and plan view were drawn with the boiler and engine positioned to the best advantage. The hull shape above the waterline is accurate, but below I had to increase the depth slightly because the boiler is of cylindrical construction and had to be set low

in the hull to allow sufficient clearance from the deck and cabin structure.

I marked in nine equally spaced bulkheads on the side elevation and plan view, and then drew two more views from the bow and stern showing the shape of each of these bulkheads. After this I was able to add the other details — cabin, engine cover, seats, etc — obtained from the slides that I had taken.

THE HULL

I made a start on the hull by cutting out plywood templates for each of the nine bulkheads and positioning them, inverted, on a bare board. The stempost, keel, propeller shaft tube and stern block were positioned and glued together, the stempost being rebated to take the planking. The

stempost and each bulkhead was then divided up to position the planking (Fig 1). I used Western Red Cedar for the hull planking as it has a straight grain and is free from knots. The initial strips were cut to 7ft x 1in x $\frac{1}{8}$in.

Starting at deck level each plank was individually fitted prior to gluing. They did not require steaming, and using epoxy resin glue two planks per side were fitted and then left to set. The planks were glued only on the edges and ends, and not intentionally to the bulkhead templates, and numerous dressmaking pins were used to hold each in place temporarily (Fig 2).

With the hull fully planked and all the pins taken out, it was removed from the baseboard with the temporary bulkheads still in position

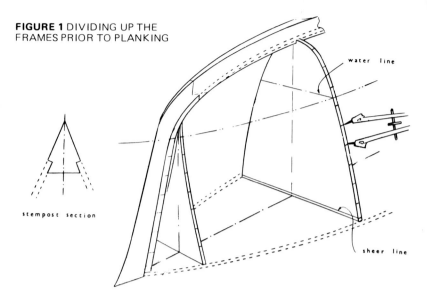

FIGURE 1 DIVIDING UP THE FRAMES PRIOR TO PLANKING

water line

stempost section

sheer line

(excess glue from each plank seam having adhered to the bulkheads). Leaving the two midship bulkheads in place, the others were removed and all excess glue was sandpapered off. The hull was now ready for the timbers (frames), which I positioned 2in apart. I made them from marine 5-ply, cutting across the grain to produce strips $\frac{5}{16}$in wide x ¼in thick. Each was then cut to length and glued in position – clothes pegs being very useful at this stage. I then removed the two remaining bulkheads and put timbers in their place; it was also necessary to fix two distance pieces across the beam to retain the correct shape.

Fine strips of fibreglass mat were then applied between each timber, which gave the hull strength and helped to retain its shape. The centreline of each timber was then transferred to the outside of the hull and, using a hand drill with a $\frac{1}{32}$in bit, I proceeded to drill holes through each plank and timber (some 1300 in all). I made $\frac{1}{32}$in dowelling from Western Red Cedar, and dipped each treenail cut from this into epoxy resin glue prior to tapping it through the hull. When set, these treenails were trimmed off inside and outside, and the outside hull surface was sanded off to a smooth finish. I next made a suitable stand for the model – remember, the hull was over 6ft long.

INTERNAL FITTINGS
The hull was now ready for the internal fitting out, and I divided this up into three main sections – bow burner, amidships the boiler

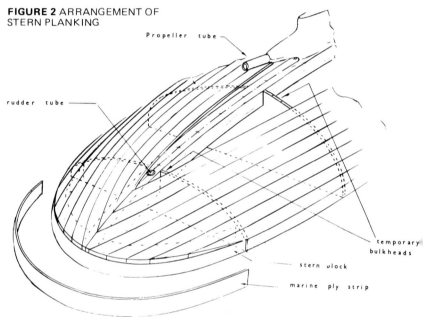

FIGURE 2 ARRANGEMENT OF STERN PLANKING

Propeller tube

rudder tube

temporary bulkheads

stern block

marine ply strip

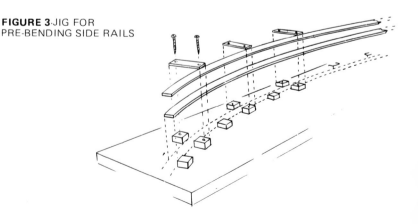

FIGURE 3 JIG FOR PRE-BENDING SIDE RAILS

and engine, and at the stern the radio compartment.

Permanent bulkheads were now cut out, the after one being positioned immediately abaft the engine and the forward one in front of the engine. I made them from marine ply, with strengthening strips across the beam; epoxy resin was used as the adhesive.

Apart from 6in at the bow and 4in at the stern the top 3in of the hull is lined with $^1/_{16}$ in marine ply fitted over the timbers. To this are glued alternate vertical strips of mahogany and Western Red Cedar. When set these were cut to length and sanded, care being necessary because of the difference in the hardness of the two woods.

The hull was now ready for the two side rails. These had to be pre-bent. They were saturated in water and steamed, after which each rail was clamped to an individual previously marked baseboard (see Fig 3). When dry and released from the boards the two rails only needed slight pressure to glue them in position on the hull. The hull and all exposed woodwork were again sanded, and the woodwork above the waterline was stained with 'English Light Oak', sanded again and sealed with polyurethane varnish.

With the upper hull sealed I was able to start work below the waterline. Setting the hull on an even keel, I marked off the waterline with scriber and block, and ran adhesive plastic masking tape along the line. The hull was then turned upside down and given an undercoat of white paint. When dry this was sanded with wet-and-dry paper and given five coats of gloss green, sanding between each coat, using plenty of water. A point to note here: if the top woodwork was not sealed at this stage it would be contaminated by the fine particles of paint from the wet and dry sanding, and these are very difficult to remove once they have been absorbed into the woodwork. When the paint was dry the masking tape was removed.

I had previously mounted the engine and boiler on to a single plate for handling and alignment purposes, and now these could be lined up with the gearbox drive which I had positioned behind the after bulkhead and coupled to the propeller shaft. From the after bulkhead to the bow I screwed a metal strip 2in wide on to the top of the keel. This was drilled and tapped to take the boiler unit, after alignment, with two $^1/_4$in diameter bolts.

With the boiler and burner being enclosed I decided to insulate these sections of the hull. I had acquired

Left: the planked hull, before the treenails had been trimmed off.
Right: the temporary plywood bulkheads in place on the baseboard, together with the stem and keel.

two cast-off photographic developing tanks, which, though corroded on the base, produced from their sides $\frac{1}{16}$in stainless steel sheets some 2ft x 2ft in size. I cut four templates from cardboard of the same thickness as the stainless steel to the hull shape, cut the steel from these, and sprang them into place after insulating the spaces between the timbers with $\frac{1}{4}$in Kaowool blanket — a ceramic fibre which compresses to $\frac{1}{8}$in thickness and which can be cut with scissors. The edges of the stainless steel sheet were then fibreglassed with tape to make a good seal (see Fig 4). I also insulated the after bulkhead with Kaowool and covered the forward side with an aluminium sheet.

The second stage was the construction of the boiler and engine cover, the cabin, the bow grating and the seats. The boiler and engine cover consisted of a frame

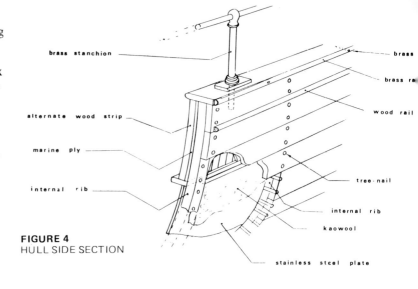

FIGURE 4
HULL SIDE SECTION

Below left: the planked and timbered hull ready for the strips of fibreglass mat to be fitted.

Top right: the port side of the engine casing, showing use of different coloured woods. Note the brass deck fittings.
Bottom right: the after cabin. The wash hand basin can be seen through the forward window.

FIGURE 5 CABIN WINDOW CORNER INSERTS

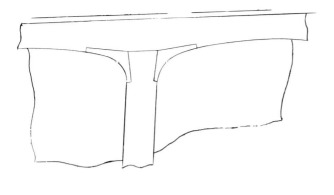

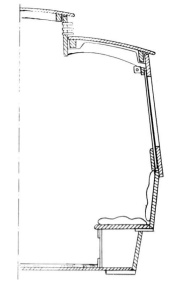

FIGURE 7 CABIN HALF SECTION

curtain
outline

ventilators

felt
carpet

sliding   door

tile   floor

FIGURE 6
CABIN HALF SECTION

for the seats, the cupboards and the toilet box section. The wash hand basin I made from the base of an aluminium aerosol spray can which, being partially domed, needed a minimum of beating to increase the size and flatten the sides to produce the flat top face. The pump handle was made from dowel turned on a hand drill and was positioned on top of a brass base alongside the basin. The floor in the forward part of the cabin has black and white tiles placed diagonally. I simulated these by cutting ¼in x ¼in squares from two polished sheets of black and white plastic ⅛in thick and 6in square. Using epoxy glue I fastened each alternate piece on to a floor template cut from 1mm ply. When dry the floor and template were trimmed and glued to the cabin floor – see Figs 6 and 7. All the cabin woodwork was then sanded, stained with 'English Light Oak', and sealed with polyurethane varnish.

To give the wood panelling depth the corners and rebated edges were shaded with light brown paint (Humbrol), blending it away towards the centre of the panels. This gives the necessary aged look and depth, and was used also on other pieces of panelling elsewhere on the hull. The roof of the cabin I painted white,

with side and end panels of ¹/₁₆in marine ply, to which I glued alternately the vertical strips of coloured woods. I made this section detachable in one piece between the forward and after bulkheads. The interior was insulated with Kaowool paper 2mm thick and covered with thin aluminium sheet.

The cabin was difficult to construct because of the slope and taper of the sides, and I so built it that it could be removed in one piece completely from the hull. As the floor of the cabin was at water level, there was enough room below it for the radio and the reversing gearbox. The sides of the cabin,

each with three windows, have wood inserts at each top corner (see Fig 5) and were prefabricated on a flat development view of the side in question. The forward and after ends of the cabin, the doors, and the internal partition were built as separate sections and when set were sanded and trimmed. In the cabin sides the perspex windows have been made to slide in channels and fit flush on the inside. The roof of the cabin is made in three removable sections to give access to the interior of the cabin. The roof lining is of marine ply on a mahogany frame.

When the various sections had been glued together I added the bases and sanded it with wet-and-dry; I gave it three coats of gloss, and after sanding the last coat an even matt finish was attained. I secured the roof to the cabin structure by means of brass swivel clips.

The floor of the after cabin was covered with green felt to represent the carpet. The seats I made in the same way as those for the bow section, which will be described later on. The end doors of the cabin are hinged with vertical pins at the top and bottom corners (see Fig 8) and the internal door slides in two metal channels, the top one being detachable so that the door can be removed.

The final removable section is the bow unit, which consists of bench-type seats over lockers, and a grating-type deck with a table. This section was constructed around a framework which was built up in position in the hull. I made the grating in halves (see Fig 9) and after trimming the edges I glued it in place. The seat bases and lockers were next completed and they, and the deck gratings, were stained and sealed with polyurethane varnish.

The seats themselves I made as follows. First I made a wood template for each one, and cut the pattern into the top surface with a sanding disc in an electric drill. I then covered each one with imitation antique leather bonded to the wood with a contact adhesive. The buttons are the heads of brass silk pins (as used in dressmaking), the excess being cut off after they had been pushed through the wood. Once the seats had been glued in place the buttons were painted brown (Fig 10).

There are two steering wheels, one in the bow section and one in the cabin. I made the spokes from beech, turning them on an electric drill (speed 900rpm), and also used beech for the outer rim, which I made in six segments. I turned the hub on the drill, and this had the spoke locating pins drilled in. Two brass rings, with locating pins soldered to them, were attached to the front and back of each wheel. A hub centre piece of brass completed each one, after which they were stained with Burmese Teak and sealed with polyurethane varnish – see Fig 11.

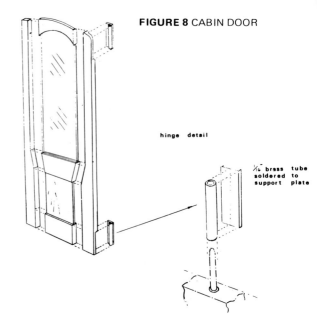

FIGURE 8 CABIN DOOR

hinge detail

¼ʺ brass tube soldered to support plate

FIGURE 9
GRATING CONSTRUCTION

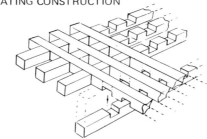

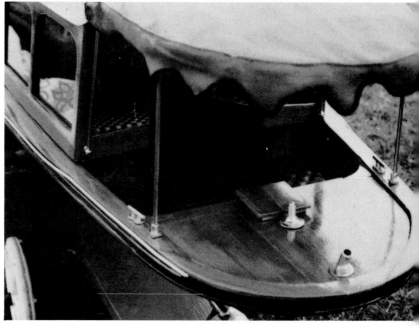

The stern, complete with canopy. Note the black and white floor covering in the cabin.

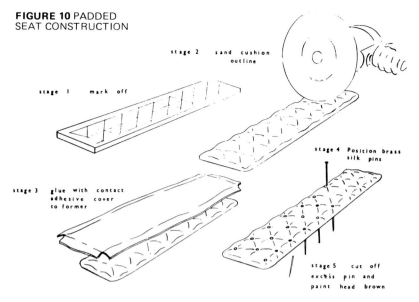

FIGURE 10 PADDED
SEER CONSTRUCTION

stage 2   sand cushion
outline

stage 1   mark off

stage 4 Position brass
silk pins

stage 3 glue with contact
adhesive cover
to former

stage 5   cut off
excess pin and
paint head brown

FIGURE 11 STEERING WHEEL CONSTRUCTION

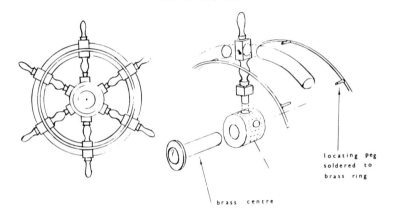

locating peg
soldered to
brass ring

brass centre

FIGURE 12 DROP LEAF TABLE

hinge detail

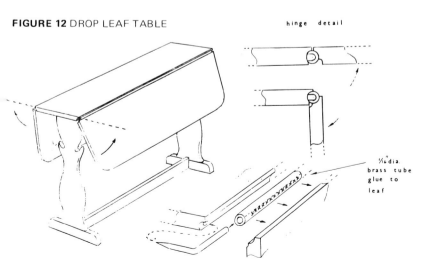

¹⁄₁₆″ dia.
brass tube
glue to
leaf

The drop leaf table in the bow section I made from Western Red Cedar. Each leaf can be raised, being hinged at each end (Fig 12). After staining and sealing, the table was glued in place on the deck grating.

The various fittings such as handrails, stanchions, cleats, etc are all made of brass. The handrail bosses and stanchions were first drilled to take the handrail and then shaped on the electric drill with files. The rails are soft-soldered to the boss of the stanchion. The canopy has a metal grid framework supported by two brass posts. I used fine green linen for the canopy itself, and stitched this to the edge of the framework. There are two flagstaffs on the model, one at the bow and one at the stern, and the latter flies the Blue Ensign.

The work on the hull was completed by painting on the name scroll and the decorative lines on the bow.

THE POWER PLANT

The power plant consisted of four units – boiler, burner, engine and gearbox. The boiler is of the centre flue type with diagonal cross tubes with the steam superheated in the flue pipe. With the funnel being forward on the engine cover the flue exhaust had to be redirected forward along the top of the boiler – this can be seen in Fig 13. After boiler pressure tests had been completed I lagged the outside with Kaowool insulating paper and covered this with strips of mahogany held in place with brass bindings. I fitted a water tank alongside the boiler, and fastened it to the hull insulating plate with self-tapping screws. Inside the tank is a hand operated water pump, access to this being gained through a hinged lid. This tank is used to fill and replenish the boiler; in half an hour the boiler used ½in depth of water.

The engine is a Stuart Turner Double Ten with Stephenson link reversing gear. I made all this from pre-machined parts. An oil box has been added to provide a drip feed to the main bearings and the eccentric end cams.

The reversing gearbox, seen in Fig 14, has been designed for radio control and also to reduce the level of the propeller shaft. The gears came from an old Sturmey Archer type three-speed bicycle unit, and were brazed on to the drive and output shafts without any apparent detrimental damage to the gear teeth. The box was test run on an electric drill and could not be faulted. The method of reversing worked very well, and will mesh and change direction with little effort.

The burner unit (Fig 15) is paraffin-fired with two blowlamp heads brazed on to a common block, and with a 4in extension tube to the standard tank, which is fitted in a horizontal position, the internal tube of the tank being repositioned to the bottom corner. The two venturi cone end covers were cut off and replaced with one large cone, which provides ample heat. With a half-pint tank it will burn for up to 30 minutes.

In practice the boiler is steamed up and the burner tank refilled prior to sailing. Due to the heat emanating from the burner a cone-shaped screen was positioned at the front of the flue tube. A screw-down type needle valve is used to control the steam supply. The radio servo is fitted direct on to the valve spindle, and a 15° movement from closed is sufficient to produce economical steaming and scale running speed.

The balanced rudder, which has a surface area of 14 sq in, required a more robust servo action, so an aircraft-type self-centring 're-tract' servo was used for this. The speed is slow but is proportional and does not overload the servo. The radios and servos are situated under the after cabin section.

The propeller is 3in in diameter, with 10in pitch, three-bladed and made from brass. The blades were cut from 1/8in brass sheet, then shaped and put into a metal jig prior to being brazed to the boss. The pitch was obtained by bending a piece of heavy gauge wire round a 3in diameter tube, one revolution per 10in length, then placing the wire over the jig and positioning each blade in turn to line up with the wire template. Some final minor adjustments were twisted into the blades after brazing. After brazing each blade was filed and then polished.

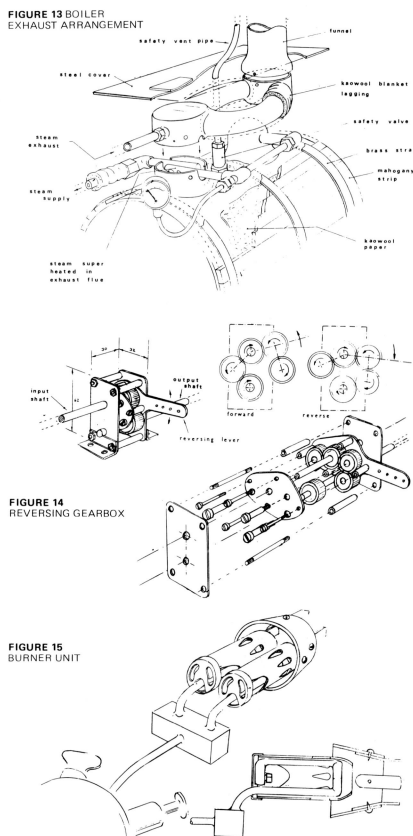

FIGURE 13 BOILER EXHAUST ARRANGEMENT

safety vent pipe

funnel

steel cover

kaowool blanket lagging

safety valve

brass strap

mahogany strip

steam exhaust

steam supply

kaowool paper

steam super heated in exhaust flue

input shaft

output shaft

reversing lever

forward

reverse

FIGURE 14 REVERSING GEARBOX

FIGURE 15 BURNER UNIT

TRIALS

The first sailing trials came one evening under calm conditions on the local park lake. I had intended only to run the engine under load, and to check the draught with the simulated weight of the cabin, engine cover, bow section and radio equipment. The model floated perfectly with no additional ballast being required; it was on an even keel and to the correct waterline. With the boiler steamed up the steam supply valve was opened just enough to run the engine at 25psi pressure. Somewhat apprehensively I decided to try a free sail – the results were beyond expectations! The next half hour was spent sailing from corner to corner of the lake. With two years work behind me, the satisfaction I felt when seeing the model sailing for the first time will long be remembered.

THE STEAM LAUNCH
BRANKSOME
Built 1896.
Builders Brockbanks of Windermere
Boiler Locomotive type, side fired
Engine Compound, bore 7½in and 11in, stroke 7in
Speed 14mph
Dimensions Length 50ft, beam 9ft

Top: the timber-covered boiler, showing the redirected exhaust flue to the funnel and the Stuart Double Ten engine.
Bottom: looking aft, showing the forward steering wheel, the panelling along the inside of the hull, and the drop-leaf table.
All uncredited photographs by John Bowen

HALF-MODELS AND HALF-MODELLING

by Keith Hobbs

The many sided facets of ship modelling have varying appeal to different model builders, so it is to those who receive most pleasure from building and shaping the hull that this aspect of the craft will have greatest appeal. However, all who admire the lines of a vessel be it large or small, ship or boat, or who wish for a diversion from the intricate and meticulous building of a complete model, may find work on a half-model both enjoyable and satisfying. Limited only by his imagination, the craftsman has an endless variety of subjects and a number of methods in producing their miniature replicas.

SOME GENERAL OBSERVATIONS
In view of their importance in ship- and boatbuilding, it is surprising so few facts concerning them have been recorded. Perhaps, as is the case with many trades and crafts, it was because of their commonplace that no one ever thought it necessary to document anything about them, so that these notes on their history and development have been taken from various sources where their mention has often been incidental, and I certainly do not wish to imply that they are completely authoritative or comprehensive. I don't doubt that some readers are better acquainted with them than I; in which case I hope they will be persuaded to put pen to paper and so add to our general knowledge.

Originally, half-models were shaped by eye without recourse to plans or drawings and it was from these that the full scale ships were built. Experience dictated the form the model should take in order that the vessel constructed on its lines would displace the desired draught of water and perform all the functions required of it. This was an art of the first order for, in a great many instances, not only was the wood shaped to a graceful form with aesthetic appeal, but it had to be essentially practical.

Some difference of opinion exists as to the introduction and general usage of the solid carved half-model. However, in the first half of the eighteenth century, a built-up type using half cross sections with ribands or stringers was usual. In England these bracket models were known as 'bird's nest' and in North America as 'Hawk's nest'. To an extent they were not unlike Dockyard models cut vertically fore and aft along the centreline.

In his book *Fast Sailing Ships 1775–1875,* David MacGregor says that these bracket models 'permitted the deadwood, transoms, knightheads and cant frames to be clearly indicated. Nineteenth century examples of the bracket model in Great Britain have been traced to Robert Steel & Co's yard at Greenock (1800–1835); to Joseph White of Cowes who used such a model for his yacht *Waterwitch* (1834); to Upton's yard at Brixham where they were in use for about ten years from the mid-fifties; to William Ferres on Restronguet Creek near Truro who designed with them from 1867–77; and to Aldous of Brightlingsea who used them for his smacks and yachts. They were also used in Holland.'

The 'lift' type composed of horizontal planks, frequently of different coloured woods dowelled together, were the most common in both Britain and North America during the nineteenth century and, as with draughts, they usually showed the starboard side. From these laminations, when taken apart, it was easy to transfer their dimensions to the drawing board or mould loft floor.

Almost certainly this latter type came about as a result of the quest for speed when naval architects and shipwrights were experimenting with new designs and breaking away from the conventional and traditional system of confining their ships to the rigid rules governing the 'midship bend'. This system had always caused problems with the bow and stern, as arcs drawn with compasses or trammels usually resulted in 'unfairness' in these sections and were left to the shipwright to fair with his adze. These complex logarithmic curves of varying radius necessary to produce the free-flowing lines at the vessel's extremities were solved with the introduction of the half-model.

Experience and experiment governed the shaping of the model with both builder and owner combining their ideas. When the design was agreed upon, the lines, taken from the 'lift' could readily be produced on paper and work on the vessel itself commenced.

The bracket type, on the other hand, would be necessarily the

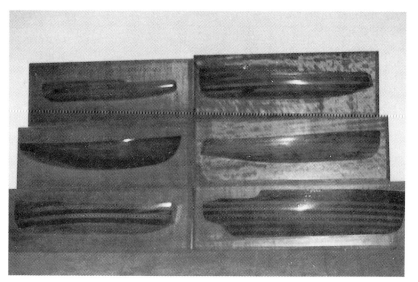

relative simplicity, the half-model offers a compromise. This is not to say they are simple to make, since, to show the true shape of the prototype, the same care as carving and contouring a complete hull is needed; but, naturally, only half the work is involved.

MOSQUIDOBID

I had not taken an especial interest in half-models until last year when I was fortunate enough to be shown some of the famous American museums (and other places of interest where many examples exist) by Merritt Edson, secretary of the Nautical Research Guild. A number of factors influenced me, not least of which were two nineteenth century examples in Mr Edson's home and, on my return, I decided to devote some attention to the subject.

To begin with I selected the American privateer schooner *Lynx* from H I Chapelle's book, *The Baltimore Clipper*. His plans are so renowned that they can be used with complete confidence knowing that, accurately executed, one will have a faithful replica of the original.

Captured by the Royal Navy in 1813, *Lynx* was renamed HMS *Mosquidobid* — no doubt in deference to those nocturnal pests infesting the coastal waterways of Florida! — and sent to England where her lines were taken off at Portsmouth in 1816. Chapelle regards her as 'a vessel worthy of very close study, as she is a fine example of the general type of privateer schooners built on the "pilot boat" model during the war of 1812'. He continues: 'This beautiful vessel is an example of the highest development of the Baltimore Clipper ...'

My introduction to the fast sailing craft of the last century built along the shores of Chesapeake Bay immediately gave rise to thoughts of

product of a draught or plan drawn first. This form of model could be useful in showing a prospective client the proposed vessel's appearance and also 'prove the lines' to the designer. Any unfairness would become apparent and so rectified on the model. The resultant more accurate lofting would economise on both timber and labour.

Nevertheless, in spite of the early convention for designing a ship based on the midship bend, the method of drafting from models was not unknown in the time of Samuel Pepys. He is known at one time to have made the following comment: 'Our own Mr Page of Wivenhoe, Bailey of Bristol (both famous for building good sailors), and old Mr Shish at Deptford are well known to be, who all depend upon their eyes, the two former never pretending to the laying down of a draught, their knowledge lying in their minds so confusedly, so as they were not able themselves to render it to anybody else but showing that the truth of shipbuilding does not lie in the niceness of lines but accommodating of a shape so as best to take in all the variety of uses we are led to desire in a ship.'

Essentially a pragmatist, the shipwright, in fashioning a half-model from which evolved a vessel to both delight the eye and perform its allotted tasks efficiently, was at once artist, designer and creator.

Although present-day shipbuilding

is more a science than an art, half-models are still used in many yards to show the location of all external plates. Not all models were mere tools of trade, however. In recent years they have been made to illustrate in three dimensions the form of a particular ship either for study or decoration. Many famous yacht clubs have displays of members' craft beautifully executed in this manner. For the model shipwright it is the pure satisfaction of seeing lines on paper come to life.

Whereas complete models take up floor or shelf space, half-models, like pictures, can be hung on a wall where, if displayed at a suitable height, their lines uncluttered by detail may be studied more easily than a model on a stand.

It is not uncommon to see some half-models with superstructure, masts and funnel or even sails. In certain examples these can look very effective. Sometimes these are mounted on a mirror in an endeavour to give the illusion of a full model. Personally, I regard this attempted deception with distaste. As with all things, one should know when to stop and I think this is particularly so with half-models. Too much detail can spoil their charm. If one wants minutiae then a full model is called for.

Most of us would like to build more models than any one person is physically capable of doing in one short lifetime. Because of their the equally rakish rig and sleek hulls of the Arabian dhows upon which, for some time, I've been trying to collect information. Unfortunately, little technical information on them appears to exist. However, there are some excellent photographs in various publications and I am looking forward to using some of these in the manner suggested by D G Bennett in his description on 'scaling from photographs' which appeared in *Model Shipwright* 27. But to return to *Mosquidobid* . . .

My first task was to transfer the published lines to the drawing board and decide on a scale. It is, of course, possible to have this done photographically but one must beware of distortion in printing.

To begin with I deducted 5ft 6in at the stern and 2ft 10in at the stem from the given 'Length on deck, 94ft 7in'. These bow and stern measurements were as near as I could ascertain from the scale on the published plan. Deducting these two amounts from 94ft 7in gave 86ft 3in and this, divided by the 23 spaces between the stations, gave 3ft 9in. This I felt was the correct spacing and I considered the combined deduction fore and aft of 8ft 4in must be right also. It might be an inch less aft and an inch

more forward but it was inconceivable that there would be spacing of say 3ft 9$\frac{1}{32}$in for example so a length of 86ft 3in sounded logical. Thus satisfied, I now began on my own draught.

First I decided on a scale of $\frac{1}{8}$in = 1ft and it was fairly straightforward to transfer the lines from book to board. By trial and error I adjusted my proportional dividers so that a given measurement on the plan produced a corresponding amount on my own drawing. I made the waterplanes 2ft 3in apart on the sheer plan and showed all these on the half breadth and body plans.

On completion of my drawings templates were cut from offcuts of acrylic sheet I purchased cheaply from a local manufacturer. This material I found to be excellent for the purpose as the templates were easy to compare with the drawing and trim off as necessary using garnet or aluminium oxide paper glued to a few suitable curved and flat sticks. These same templates were used in fairing up my drawing, thus testing the accuracy of both.

For the hull I used pieces of Queensland red cedar I'd had lying about for years. These had to be cut and planed to the scale thickness of the waterplanes – 2ft 3in. Unless one

has sophisticated equipment, this is easier said than done, and for my next model I had timber thicknessed at the timber yard first and then made my waterplanes to suit.

Having eventually succeeded in preparing my timber I cut out each waterplane using its corresponding template. A bandsaw is useful for this but a hand-held coping saw would do as long as it was cut carefully at right angles. To assist in later carving one must make sure the grain of each lamination runs the same way. On the subject of grain it is perhaps worth bearing in mind that planks warp away from the heart wood and could cause edges to open up. Cutting out the centre should help eliminate this tendency and would be advisable for large scale work.

On each waterplane also the cross sections were also marked and, when gluing up, care was needed to match these and keep the centreline flat, coinciding with each successive layer. Two at a time were tackled — more would probably have resulted in the middle one slipping off line. When all the planks were glued together I screwed them to a flat piece of plywood the shape of the profile. To this I glued a scrap piece of wood for holding in a vice.

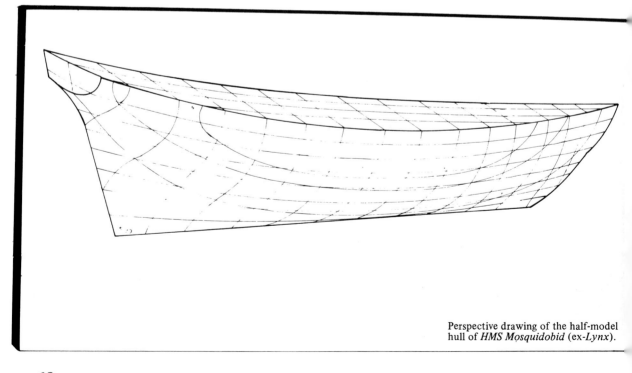

Perspective drawing of the half-model hull of *HMS Mosquidobid* (ex-*Lynx*).

Top: Neil Cormack's half-model of the 4-mast barque *Herzogin Cecilie*.
Centre: the bow of the half-model of the *Herzogin Cecilie*.
Bottom: the after end of the *Herzogin Cecilie* half-model.

All photographs by the author

The top plank was then trimmed to shape. The sheer should be at right angles with the base, which should show each section and waterplane. This plywood also served to strengthen the fine ends as I worked. Care should be taken to leave the waterplanes untouched. There is a temptation to take the odd shaving off as sometimes the half section templates seem to indicate this.

Provided the waterplanes are cut accurately and the plank thickness is also correct, common sense dictates that they must remain constant and any paring away here will be wrong. In carving under the counter I did not heed my own advice and I stupidly pared away a little too much with the result that I had to insert a thin fillet along the centreline to compensate for this. This solved the difficulty but it should not have occurred in the first place. Sectional templates must be held perpendicular to the base and by rubbing chalk on their inside edge I was able to see the high spots; sighting into the light and marking these places also assisted. At the ends the hull diminished to a 'feather' edge and, in spite of the brittle cedar, I experienced no trouble with breakage due to the firmly held plywood base backing.

When the hull was shaped to my satisfaction, I put it to one side and then cut veneer thin pieces for the keel, stem, sternposts and rudder. If the scale one is working to warrants it, then the posts and rudder should be shown with the correct

taper, ie the rudder and sternpost have a slightly greater siding at the top, and vice versa for the stem. With these pieces lightly glued to a scrap of plywood I marked out the profile and cut them out as shown, afterwards removing them – water soluble glue with a piece of newspaper between helps – and carefully gluing to a previously prepared baseboard.

The hull was then removed from the plywood and positioned and screwed on the baseboard. Because this was on the posts and keel a strip of the same wood was placed along the top to compensate. The marginally increased beam which resulted would be approximately

Above: the author's half-model of HMS *Mosquidobid* (ex-*Lynx*).

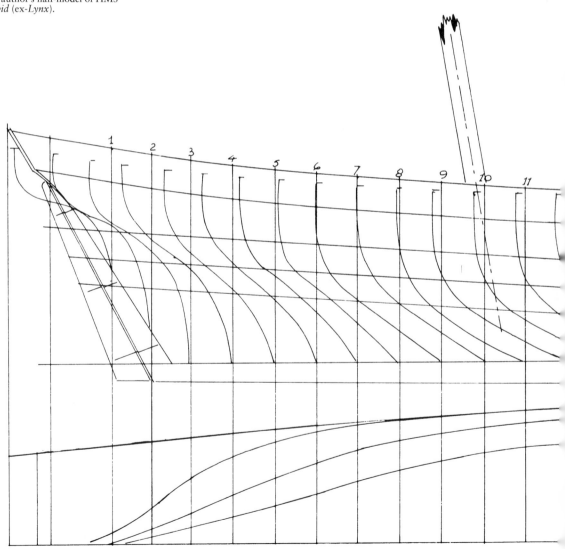

the thickness of the planking as the lines are to the outside of the frames. At this scale, to have fitted the posts and keel around the hull would have been unnecessary. A builder's half-model would not show them.

The dark, reddish-brown cedar contrasted pleasingly with the light, honey-coloured base. Mast stumps and the bowsprit were also shown. The foremast, incidentally, is raked more than the main; the fact that they seem parallel is an optical illusion which misled Chapelle (see page 82 of *The Baltimore Clipper*).

I gave the finished work a liberal coat of beeswax diluted with pure turpentine and, after

Above: another view of the half-model of *Mosquidobid*, taken at an angle of 45°.

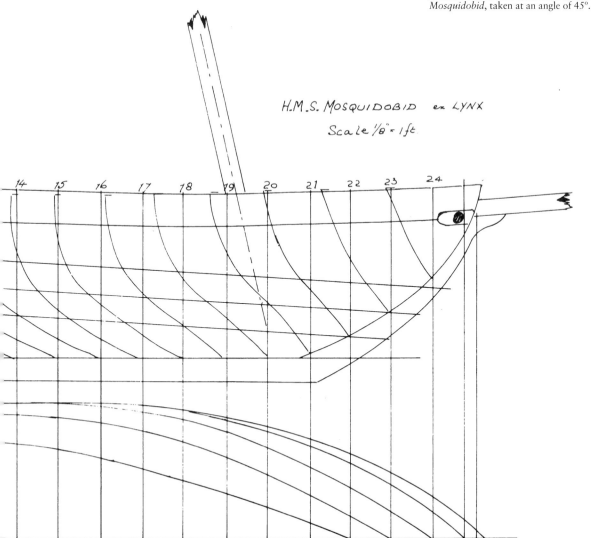

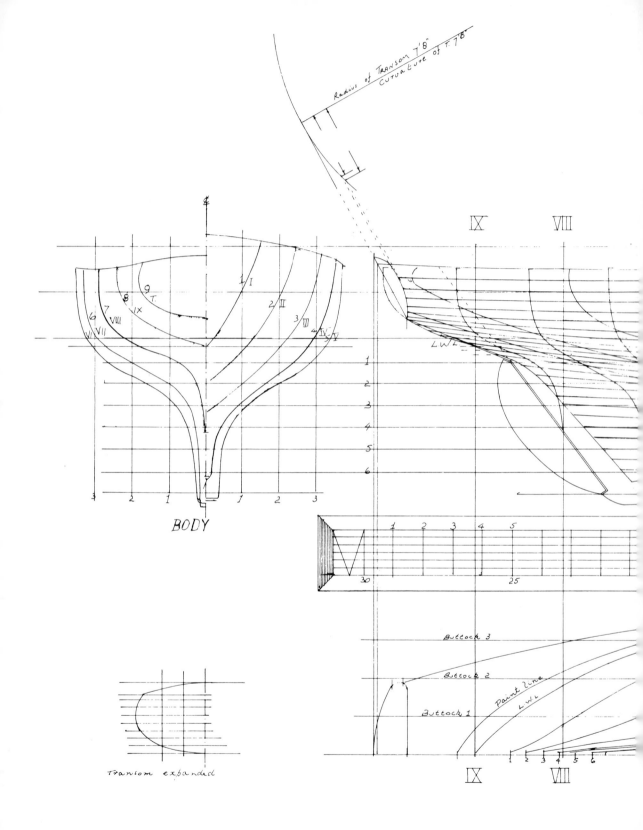

Radius of Transom 7'8"
Curvature of T. 7'8"

IX   VIII

LWL

BODY

Transom expanded

Buttock 3

Buttock 2

Buttock 1
Paint Line
LWL

IX   VIII

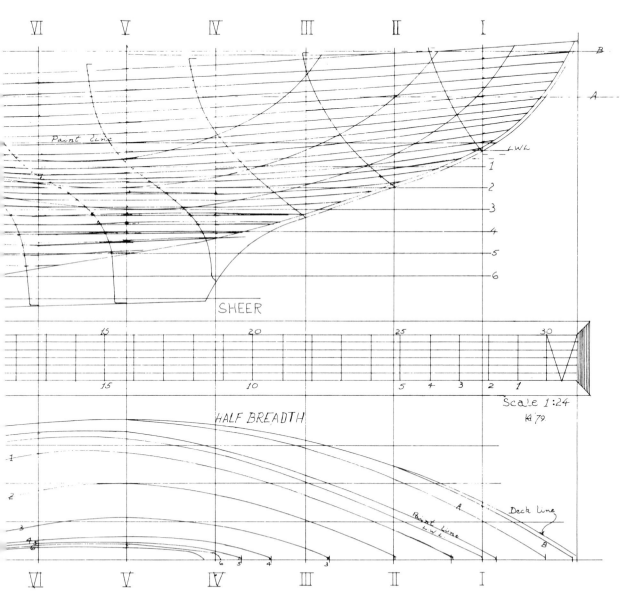

VI   V   IV   III   II   I

B

A

Paint line

LWL
1
2
3
4
5
6

SHEER

15   20   25   30

15   10   5 4 3 2 1

Scale 1:24
KI 79

HALF BREADTH

1

2

3

4
5
6

A   Deck line

Paint line
LWL   B

6 5   4   3

VI   V   IV   III   II   I

NOONGARA   — Captain D P Manthorpe, Adelaide

L.O.A. 30'07"   L.W.L. 24'00"

Beam 9'1¾"   Draught 5'02"

Lines taken from builders blans & reduced to ½"=1ft.

allowing time for it thoroughly
to soak in, polished it to a soft
sheen.

MOONGARA

A yacht hull was one of the types
which interested me so, the
builder's lines being available, my
next project was a friend's yacht.

Perhaps a brief history of this
vessel might be of interest. She is
a sloop-rigged *Blythe Spirit* class
vessel designed by L A Randell of
Perth, Western Australia, and the
first of her class was built in Sydney
in 1959. The hull is carvel-built of
Queensland beech planking on
laminated timbers of stringy bark,
copper-nailed and roved. Her name,
Moongara, is southern Aboriginal
tribal dialect meaning 'soul' or
'spirit'. Her particulars are:
Length oa 30ft 10½in, beam 9ft 2in
and light draught 5ft 3in, giving a
displacement of 5.5 tons.

A dedicated yachtsman of many
years experience as well as being a
professional seaman, her owner has
cruised extensively in the Great
Australian Bight and the waters of
the Nuyts Archipelago and has
undertaken a protracted cruise to
New Zealand, Tonga, the Fijian
Islands, New Caledonia and the
Queensland Barrier Reef, some
9300 miles in all.

Knowing a model of this vessel
would be subject to the most
stringent criticism encouraged me
to take special care. To begin with
I reduced the scale from 1in = 1ft
to ½in = 1ft from the original line
plan and cut all my templates from
¹/₁₆ in perspex as before. When these
were faired to my satisfaction, I
redrew my plan using these
templates to draw smooth curves
as I wished to present my friend with
the drawing on completion of the
model.

By recent good fortune I had been
able to acquire some Tasmanian Huon
pine which is difficult to come by
nowadays. The popularity of this
famous timber and the resultant
indiscriminate felling has caused its
present shortage. In the past it was
widely used in boat- and shipbuilding
and, having heard so much about it
over the years, I was anxious to try
it on a suitable project. What better,
I thought, than this yacht. I decided

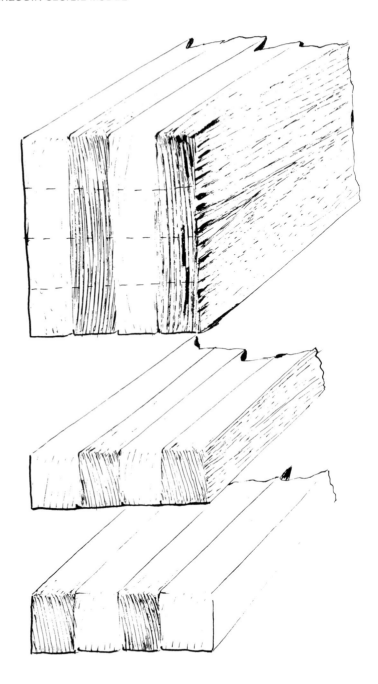

to do below the 'paint line' in this
light yellow wood and, above it, use
myrtle beech, another beautiful
Tasmanian timber, which is very
hard with a fine close grain which
cuts well, polishes easily and has a
pleasing light red colour. Learning
from my previous experience, I had
the wood machine thicknessed and

then used this thickness to establish
my waterplanes. The pine worked
beautifully and also took a good
polish. It is of fine texture and
medium in hardness. To complete
the job I mounted it on a board of
Queensland red cedar and presented
it to my friend along with a lines
plan and sectional templates so he

could test the accuracy of my work!

Many of the yacht hull models which grace club houses throughout the world are painted. To do this I suggest that the waterplanes be screwed and dowelled together enabling later dis-assembly for painting. A waterline may be shown by inserting a thin plank between the boot-topping and the topsides. On completion of carving, the grain should be filled, undercoated and rubbed down until a good base is prepared. The model can then be separated and the colours painted. When re-assembled, the demarcation lines should be perfectly straight.

If one wishes, as an alternative method of construction to horizontal waterplanes, vertical planks cut to the shape of the bow and buttock lines may be used. Instead of different coloured woods to accentuate the various planes, black photographic paper or similar material could be inserted between the planes and the finished model would show them as fine black lines. A combination showing all sections and planes as shown in the sketch could be done but would need access to precision sawing and planing.

Another interesting variation is that shown in the photograph of a half-model of the famous four-masted barque *Herzogin Cecilie* built at Geestemunde in 1902 and for many years on the Australian grain trade. This particular half-model was made by Mr Neil Cormack, senior shipwright surveyor for the Department of Marine and Harbours in South Australia. His method was to cut the timber into vertical sections, each being equal to the spacing of the bow and buttock lines. Using alternate light and dark woods, he glued them together and, when the glue was set, cut the resulting block into the horizontal planes. Each alternate plane was then turned over so the dark wood of one layer was above the light wood of the other. These were then shaped according to their individual planes in the usual method. This would result in each lamination having the grain reversed so care would need to be taken in working. In each of the two latter methods showing the bow and buttock lines, these, if fair and true, further demonstrate the accuracy of one's work.

Some models include the wales and are planked, with headrails and quarter-galleries also shown. Others are of the bracket type partly planked with all frames inserted. An unusual model is in Independence Hall, Philadelphia, showing Humphrey's model of a projected 74-gun ship of the Revolution. From a photograph it appears to be placed on a kind of an easel which can be raised or lowered. This example shows headrails, quarter-galleries and bowsprit. Truly, there are many variations on the theme!

REFERENCES

MacGregor, D R: *Fast Sailing Ships*
Chapelle, H I: *The Search for Speed under Sail*
Chapelle, H I: *The National Watercraft Collection*
Chapelle, H I: *The Baltimore Clipper*
Chapelle, H I: *The American Sailing Navy*
Half Modelling (Bath Marine Museum, Bath, Maine, USA.)
The Mariners' Mirror (Society for Nautical Research)
The Nautical Research Journal (Nautical Research Guild)

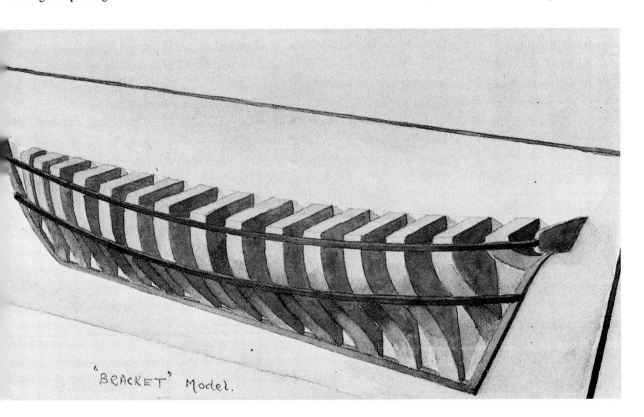

'BRACKET' Model.

Empress to

by Jack Claridge

The *Empress of Japan* was the second of a famous trio of vessels built for the Canadian Pacific Railway Company to run from Vancouver to Hong Kong. These three steamers — the *Empresses of India, Japan* and *China* — were destined to make history on the Pacific Ocean. The CPR had been given a contract to carry the mails across Canada, thence across the Pacific, and the stipulated transit time from Halifax or Quebec to Vancouver and on to Hong Kong was not to exceed 28½ days in summer or 30½ days in winter, with heavy cash penalties for late departures or arrivals. Three fast steamers would be required to maintain the schedule, and, in return for a substantial annual subsidy, they were to have a trial speed of 17kts and a sea speed of 16kts, and were to be designed as auxiliary cruisers, provided with gun platforms, and built to Admiralty-approved specifications. The contract for the three vessels, signed on 12 October 1889, went to the Naval Construction and Armament Company of Barrow-in-Furness.

The ships were particularly graceful in appearance. Their length between perpendiculars was 455.6ft, but the counter stern and clipper bow increased their overall length to slightly over 485ft. With a beam of 51.2ft, a moulded depth of 36ft, a draught of 24½ft, a gross tonnage of 5940 tons and a loaded displacement of 11,750 tons, they were large ships by contemporary standards. The builders were asked to guarantee a trial speed of 18kts, this to be provided by two independent triple expansion engines, installed in separate engine rooms, each driving a separate propeller. Twin screws were still a novelty in 1889, and

the *Empresses* were the only twin-screw steamers in the trans-Pacific trade for the following decade. This was certainly an important safeguard against disaster on the long run to the Orient, in unfrequented waters, long before the days of wireless, where a disabled steamer might drift helplessly for weeks without being sighted.

No reasonable expense was spared to make the *Empresses* capable of maintaining the service for which they were designed. In the light of modern-day figures, it is interesting to note the cost of these three ships was $3,471,587, or slightly more than $1,157,000 each, an amount which today would not pay for a small tug or fishing trawler.

The first of the trio, the *Empress of India*, had her keel laid in November 1889, was launched on 30 August 1890, and ran her trials in January 1891, when she reached a speed of 18.65kts. Her trial trip was the first time the red and white chequer-board house flag of the CPR (designed by the company's President, Sir William van Horne) was ever hoisted. The second ship, the *Empress of Japan*, was launched on 13 December 1890 and proved slightly faster, her speed on the measured mile being 18.91kts. The last of the trio, *Empress of China*, was launched on 25 March 1891 and ran her trials in July. Though she registered a full 19kts on the measured mile, she was never able to equal that mark, while her subsequent performance in service proved she was neither the fastest nor the most economical of the three sisters.

The *Empress of India* left Hong Kong on 17 April 1891, inaugurating the trans-Pacific service, and arrived at Victoria on 28 April, a land-to-

the Orient

Below: this view of the *Empress of Japan*, c1903, shows a wealth of useful modelling detail — the run of the strakes of shell plating, the figurehead, the hawse pipes, the bowsprit rigging, and many other forecastle and foremast details.

land record of 11 days, 7 hours, 27 minutes; this was reduced to 10 days, 21 hours, 23 minutes, however, by the *Empress of Japan* on her maiden voyage two months later. The *Empress of China* completed her maiden voyage on 23 September 1891, and the three ships began to shuttle back and forth across the Pacific with proverbial regularity. For fifteen years, from 1891 to 1906, no *Empress* missed a sailing or was penalised for late arrival of her mails, an adherence to schedule which has probably not been equalled elsewhere.

From the first, the *Empress of Japan* proved to be slightly faster than her sisters. Her maiden voyage clipped more than 10 hours from *India*'s record, and, on her second voyage to Vancouver, she bettered this figure by more than 8 hours, arriving at Victoria from Yokohama in 10 days, 13 hours, 10 minutes, an average speed of 16.59kts. Some years later, *Japan* reduced her time to 10 days, 10 hours, and this record stood until the arrival of the new *Empress of Russia* in 1913. In 1897 the *Japan* set a westbound record, never approached by either of her

sisters, of 10 days, 3 hours, 39 minutes, at an average speed of 17.14kts, including a record run for a single day of 441 miles for an average speed of 18.4kts. These runs were unusual: for an average passage, operating at a speed of 14−15kts, the *Empresses* burned 110−120 tons of coal a day. Consumption on the round trip from Vancouver to Hong Kong usually totalled about 5500tons.

Fame and popularity came the way of the *Empresses* from their maiden voyages, due in part to the fact that they were the largest and fastest steamers trading across the Pacific, and also to their graceful appearance which seems to have caught the imagination of the travelling public. By 1897, despite the fact there were 18 ships competing for business, the *Empresses* were carrying 60 per cent of all first-class travellers across the Pacific. Homeward-bound the most important items in their cargoes were silk and tea. Speed was of cardinal importance in the transport of raw silk, and, as they offered the fastest schedule, the *Empresses* captured a large

proportion of this trade. Million dollar shipments were carried at times (an impressive figure in the 1890s), while in 1902 CPR steamers landed four silk cargoes at Vancouver within 40 days, valued at $5,941,000. Opium arrived on almost every steamer for some years, while rice was carried in large quantities. The most important items in their outward cargoes were flour and cotton goods, plus machinery and a variety of manufactured articles.

Despite strong American and Japanese competition, the *Empresses* retained their popularity to a surprising degree in the years 1900-1910. Though eventually surpassed in size and speed, they still offered the fastest regular schedule across the Pacific. The reliability of their service was legendary, considerations of great importance to the silk and tea trades; while their yacht-like lines and faster schedules (tied to through bookings across Canada by rail) accounted for their success in continuing to attract first-class passengers, this despite the fact they could be wet and

uncomfortable in a seaway. The ships could roll and pitch in an astonishing way, and on occasion threw the clinometer beyond 45 degrees, though fitting bilge keels in 1901 reduced their rolling considerably. Two other reasons for their success should not be overlooked. They were kept in first-class condition, upkeep was never stinted, and they were thoroughly overhauled each year at Hong Kong. They were, moreover, well run, and had the good fortune to attract a large number of efficient and popular officers. The names of Captains O P Marshall, Henry Pybus, Rupert Archibald, Samuel Robinson, and A J Hailey were household words in Vancouver and in the Orient.

Probably the best-known and most popular of the Empress captains was Samuel Robinson, born in hull in 1870, who joined the CPR as a junior officer on the *Empress of Japan* in 1895, becoming Chief Officer of the *Empress of China* in 1899. In 1903 he was appointed to command the *Athenian*, took over the *Monteagle* in 1906, and moved to the *Empress of Japan* in 1911. In 1913 he was sent to the Clyde to bring out the new *Empress of Asia*, and commanded the *Asia* or her sister, the *Empress of Russia*, for the next nine years. In 1922 he arrived in England to assume command of the German-built *Empress of Australia* (ex-*Tirpitz*). A year later, on 1 September, 1923, sudden and lasting fame came to the *Australia* and Captain Robinson when they were instrumental in saving more than 4000 lives in the Yokohama earthquake disaster, for which Robinson was awarded the CBE. In 1924 he commanded the *Empress of Canada* on a round-the world cruise, a rare event in those days. Following spells in the *Empress of France* and *Empress of Canada*, as senior Pacific Commander, he was appointed to bring out the new queen of the fleet, the 26,000-ton *Empress of Japan* (II) in 1929, rounding out his notable career as her commander until his retirement in 1932.

By 1910 the *Empresses* were showing signs of twenty years of hard use. Though they were equipped with wireless in 1909, no great attempt was made to up-date their passenger accommodation. In the summer of 1911, long-expected orders were placed for two new and much larger vessels, the *Empress of Russia* and the *Empress of Asia*. The assumption was that the two new liners and two old *Empresses* would maintain a fortnightly service to the Orient. Any speculation as to the fate of the third old *Empress* was promptly settled when the *Empress of China* impaled herself on a reef off the entrance to Tokyo Bay. She was so firmly embedded, it was five months before she could be refloated, and the extent of damage dictated she be abandoned to the underwriters, who disposed of her to ship-breakers.

Shortly after the outbreak of war in August 1914, the *Empress of India* was requisitioned by the Admiralty, fitted out as a hospital ship at the expense of the Maharajah of Gwalior, and renamed *Loyalty*. She had a busy wartime career, making 41 trips and carrying over 15,000 patients. After the Armistice, she served briefly as a troopship, then was sold in 1919 to the Scindia Steam Navigation Company who proposed to operate her between India, the Mediterranean, and Britain. She was refitted as a

An interesting point about this photograph of the *Empress of Japan* lying moored is that that at this stage of her life all the boats are dark brown. The aftermost boat and its davits – normally carried outboard of the shrouds to the mainmast – appear to have been temporarily removed.

passenger ship, but her period of service was brief. She was laid up in Bombay in 1921 and finally sold for scrapping in February 1923.

The *Empress of Japan* proceeded to Hong Kong when war was declared, where she was at once fitted out as an auxiliary cruiser, armed with eight old 4.7in guns, platforms for which had been provided at the time she was built. In this guise she made a number of cruises but saw little action. By the end of 1915 her services were no longer required, she was released by the Admiralty, and returned to her normal trans-Pacific duties. By 1920 it was clear the *Japan* was nearing the end of her career. The new 21,500-ton *Empress of Canada* was taking shape at Fairfields in Glasgow, though, due to delays in her completion, the old *Japan* was reprieved for a year, sailing on her final round trip to the Orient on 1 June 1922 and returning on 18 July for the last time. Few ships served their owners as well, or caused as little anxiety. She was in commission 31 years, and for 22 of them she held the Pacific record. She crossed the Pacific 315 times and steamed over 2,000,000 miles, 62,000 of which she covered while in the

Below and right: three views of the completed model.
All photographs from the author's collection.

service of the Admiralty. For four years she swung at anchor in Vancouver harbour, but was finally broken up in 1926. Her original Japanese dragon figurehead awaits restoration, though a replica has been erected at the entrance to Vancouver harbour. Her bell now lies in the Vancouver Maritime Museum, close by the author's model.

THE MODEL

I have vivid recollections of seeing the *Empress* anchored in Vancouver harbour, less than a mile from where I lived as a small boy in 1923, and I believe this memory is what first fired my enthusiasm for model ships. However, it was not until 1948 that the project actually got under way with a search for plans and photographs. As was to be expected, detailed plans of the ship could not be found, though correspondence with the builders did result in cabin plans of the various passenger decks. A fine elevation or sail plan of the ship, and the midship hull lines (presumably of use for dry-docking purposes) were obtained from Hong Kong and Whampoa Dock Co — plans which had obviously been in their files, undistrubed, for many years. Some good photographs of the *Empresses* were available locally, but a tremendous stroke of luck was seeking out and becoming friendly with Captain Samuel Robinson, then nearing 80 years of age, whose hobby during his sea-going days had been photography. His albums of photos taken on the *Empresses* were indispensable and, for the six years the model was under construction (1949–55), seldom did a month go by without a meeting with him, to

report or show progress, and to check his recollections and photographic references to ensure details were correct — a friendship which continued until his death in September 1958.

Captain Robinson also provided another invaluable source of information on hull and deck details, a copy of Volume II of *Practical Ship Building* by A Campbell Holms, printed in 1904, a book which over the years has provided answers to so many questions on iron ship construction of that general era. Included in this book was not only a layout diagram of the *Empress* (no hull lines, unfortunately), but also detailed drawings of the propeller bossing, so important to the underwater shape of these ships. With this data, it was possible to draw a set of hull lines, no real problem as the hulls of these ships were close to the latter-day moderate clipper ships, with counter sterns, clipper bows with moderate flare, plus a bowsprit.

From the hull lines and the longitudinal plan, various lifts were marked out for the hull, built on the 'bread and butter' system from ¾in planks of yellow cedar, following my usual procedures outlined in a previous article. The hull was shaped, paying particular attention to the propeller bossing and the counter stern with its knuckle, up to the main or promenade deck which is marked by a red stripe around the hull. A deck of thin plywood was installed; cabin structures on the promenade deck, hatches, poop and forecastle decks marked, and the rest of the deck marked for planks. Above this rise the bulwarks for the well decks, and the side hull structure for the enclosed promenade with its long line of port holes. At the bow is the figurehead (a Japanese dragon on the *Japan*, a bust of Queen Victoria on the *India*, and a Chinese dragon on the *China*). I made mine of plasticine which, when varnished and then painted in gay colours, looks quite realistic. Both bow and stern deck structures have modified whaleback deck areas, presumably to aid in shedding water which came aboard.

The forward cabin structure on the promenade deck is the dining saloon. On the upper deck, above the dining area, is the library with its large skylight and ornate stained glass windows which were protected by steel shutters in bad weather. Above the library was the open bridge, pilot house, chart room, etc. All decks, as can be seen from the photos, were planked including forecastle and poop decks, top of pilot house, etc. The larger of the two deckhouses on the spar or lifeboat deck was designated as the smoking room, an addition after original construction when the smoking room was one deck lower. A prominent feature is the wood framing for canvas awnings which in good weather covered most of the exposed deck area below the spar deck, from the stern forward to the bridge. Other than the canvas awning, the bridge was open and exposed to the elements for most of the ship's career, a most uncomfortable situation in bad weather for the officer on watch. Eventually, small bridge houses were built to give some protection.

While some commercial fittings were bought (such as brass stanchions, air ports, anchors, searchlight, life rings and chain), the model otherwise is built from scratch. Decks are varnished ply, lined for planking (to me an unsatisfactory process; since this model, all decking has been laid). Deckhouses are of thin ply, built around a form to get the proper curves, and stripped with ply to represent panelling, etc. As much detail as feasible was incorporated, based on a close study of hundreds of photos of the ship and her sisters, and much time was spent in obtaining correct detail. (The library, bridge, and pilot house structure, for example, took all one winter to build). The three masts are of birch, carefully tapered; funnels are brass tubing. Lifeboats are built from solid blocks of yellow cedar, hollowed, and fitted with ribs, floorboards, thwarts, oars, rudders, pike poles, masts and sails. All are white with mahogany trim except the forward pair, the sea boats, which are finished in mahogany. The sea boats and the after pair are carried in the swung-out position, the others mounted inboard on the spar deck. Cowl ventilators (and there are many of them) were made from dowel rod, shaped and sanded to size. The accommodation ladder is shown in the 'down' position on the port side, clewed up to the rail on the starboard.

As these ships were built when sail was common, they were all equipped with fore-and-aft sails on the three masts. I have represented these on the model brailed up to the gaffs and booms. Some captains used sail from time to time, most did not, and finally they were removed altogether.

COLOUR SCHEME

The three ships owed much of their popularity to their attractive colour scheme. For most of their service lives the lower hull was red, above which was a wide boot topping of pink; the main area of the hull was white, up to the top of the main deck bulwarks. At the main deck level was a noticeable stripe around the hull which on the *Japan* was red, on the *India* blue, and on the *China* green. The hull above the main deck bulwarks was tan, as were the whaleback decks fore and aft. Bowsprit, breakwater, hatch coamings, mast, booms, funnels and the main ventilators were tan (white inside the ventilator bell), though most of the small ventilators, anchors, chains, capstans, gun mountings, canvas frames, etc were white. Deck machinery was black and the forward deck under the bowsprit grey, while stairways, cap rails, library window frames and shutters, safety hand-rails, skylights, doors, flag lockers, etc were mahogany or teak. As a mail carrier, the *Empress* customarily flew the Royal Mail pennant at the forepeak, the CPR houseflag at the main, and, as her officers were invariably RNR men, the blue ensign at the stern.

The construction of this model was spread over six years, from 1949 to 1955. The scale is ⅛in = 1ft, giving an overall length of almost 61in. Total working time was in excess of 2500 hours. The model was loaned to the Vancouver Maritime Museum in 1962 for a specific exhibit, and, except for a 2-year period at the Maritime Museum of BC in Victoria, has been prominently displayed there ever since.

THE INDUSTRY

Hastings luggers are still very much part of the English South Coast scene, and although power has now superseded sail their essential design features have remained unchanged since the nineteenth century. The *Industry*, a lugger built in 1880, is the subject of **Alistair Brown**'s latest project.

The *Industry* was a typical lute-sterned, clinker-built Hastings lugger. She was just under 33ft with a very full hull shape, beamy, and with flat floors. Luggers similar in size and design can still be seen on the beach at Hastings, although sail has now given way to power. The manner of launching, and, in particular, beaching these boats on Hastings' steep, stony shore determined the construction and design of these boats to such an extent that they have remained unchanged for over a hundred years.

I first came across details of the *Industry* in 1972 when I purchased Volume 2 of Edgar March's *Inshore Craft of Great Britain*. It seemed to be a craft with more than average charm and interest, and I was

determined to construct an accurate working model at some time in the future. I postponed the project until I was sure I had sufficient skill and experience to make a good job of a clinker-built hull with many strakes. In the autumn of 1979 I was ready to start, having experimented with clinker construction in the building of the Spithead wherry *Woodham* (see *Model Shipwright* 28). I had built the *Woodham* over moulds but decided to plank the *Industry* directly on to the frames. I realise that a clinker vessel should have its hull formed by the shape of the planks and the frames added after that, but this seemed impractical as I was modelling a specific shape exactly. For that reason I built the

frames first and added the planks in the usual plank-on-frame method, only lapping the planks in this case.

THE HULL AND CABIN

The Science Museum provided small copies of Philip Oke's drawings of the *Industry*, consisting of lines, sections, sail plan and GA, including interior details. I scaled up the lines to ¾in = 1ft and drew out the frames at the positions shown in Oke's drawings. I later discovered that where these were covered by the ceiling Philip Oke had been incorrect. However, as the ceiling covers those same frames in the model it does not matter too much. I built the frames from ³/₁₆in spruce and most were double. These were then set up on the keel and the keelson added.

To support the frames the beam shelves were put in. These were ¼in square and were laminated in position from four strips each, ¹/₁₆in thick. This gave a rigid, strong support to the upper ends of the frames. I then cut and sanded the outer faces of the frames to the correct level to allow the planks to sit fairly against them. A stringer was added to the tops of the frames, and the lute stern built on to the transom.

Before planking could start I had to mark the points at which the upper edges of each plank would cross the

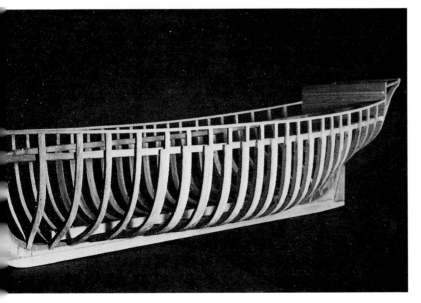

Left: *Industry* almost ready for planking. One cant frame each side was added at the bows after this photo was taken.
Derek Brown

Overleaf: the author's model of the Hastings lugger *Industry* had a very brief sailing career, and now resides in the Bembridge Maritime Museum.
John Bowen

frames. Careful study of the photographs of the *Industry* showed nineteen strakes from the keel to the rail. The bulwarks were built as a continuation of the main hull. In most Hastings luggers the clinker construction stopped at the covering board and the bulwarks were carvel-built above that. In the *Industry* there was no covering board, apparently, and the curve of the strakes was different from the sheer of the deck. The line of the scuppers can be clearly seen in photographs cut through one of the planks. It seems that the frames extended up as far as seventeen

planks, the eighteenth and nineteenth planks being supported by five very large wooden knees set up on each side of the deck. I divided each frame into seventeen sections which gave me the true run of the planks, and the hull was planked from the garboard up using these marks. After that the top two planks each side were put on, with another stringer and the rail (see Figure 1).

The next stage was to add the ceiling to the hold, the bulkheads and the interior of the cabin. The latter consisted of four bunks, lockers and a stove. The stove was built from

balsa covered with plastic card, with details also built up from plastic card. The chimney was built from the same material as far as the deck. Later, a turned aluminium piece was fitted to the deck over which fitted the removable part of the chimney, made from brass on the model. See Figure 2.

DECK FITTINGS AND PAINTING NOTES
Having fitted out and painted the interior of the hull, I added the deck beams and laid the deck. The deck consisted of $^1/_{16}$in × $^3/_{16}$in

Above: the line of scuppers referred to in the text is clearly visible in this photograph. Hull colours are black and red, with stern and interiors of bulwarks white.
John Bowen

the holes drilled out to $\frac{1}{16}$ in diameter and wooden treenails inserted. This gives the appearance of nail holes stopped with wooden discs. The mast case (tabernacle) and companionway were built up off the model and added when complete. The companionway hatch was made to open correctly so that the cabin interior could be seen to some extent. Scuppers were cut in the hull at deck level and the large knees fitted to support the bulwarks. Two large breasthooks were added to the bows, and feathers and knees put on the mast case. The feathers are large, curving timbers running from the mast case to the companionway which help support the base of the foremast as it is lowered when fishing. Tow post ('veer-away' post'), hatch coamings and capstan completed the hull, along with various metal fittings such as the gammon iron and mizzenmast bracket.

For interest's sake I decided to make the capstan work. The *Industry* carried an iron capstan which rotated around a central axle, turned by cogs

spruce planks, with black cartridge paper inserted as caulking. These were fixed with glue and pins. When the glue had set, the pins were removed,

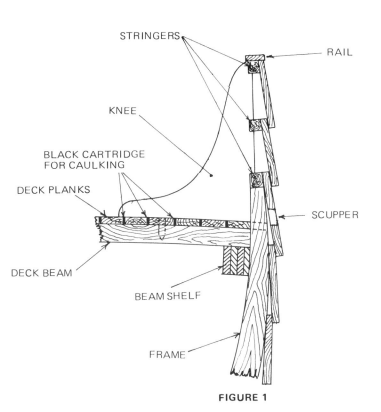

FIGURE 1

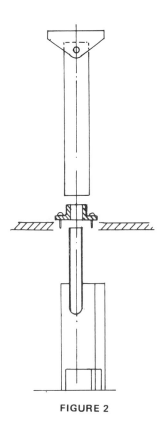

FIGURE 2

engaging teeth cut in the top of the capstan, as shown in Figure 3. I turned the body of the capstan from aluminium, leaving a ring at the top into which I filed the teeth. Figure 4 shows the various parts of the capstan.

The most difficult part was the cutting of the teeth in the top to suit the cog used. I was pleased with the result of my labours as the finished capstan worked well. However, the aluminium teeth began to wear after a while, so it was just as well that the whole model went into a glass case in a museum!

Having completed the construction of the basic hull, I painted the inside of the bulwarks white, with the supporting knees in black and then the outside of the hull in black, with a red strip each side, and the lute stern in white. To achieve a satisfactory finish I used the following method for the outside of the hull. First three coats of red oxide metal primer, sold in car accessory shops, were put on, rubbing down thoroughly between coats. That gave an excellent base. Then the whole hull, except

the lute stern, was given two coats of gloss black, followed after a few days by one coat of well-stirred matt varnish. The matt varnish tones down the gloss to a dull sheen that looks right. The white and red were mixed from 50/50 gloss/matt paints and again came out as a dull sheen. I used more or less the same technique for the interior painting except that

thinned, clear cellulose dope was applied as a primer instead of the red oxide. The dope is cleaner to work with and more easily covered, but it is less durable than the red oxide primer and the gloss paint chips off it more easily. All 'unpainted' wood was given an initial coat of matt varnish to which had been added some dark brown and grey

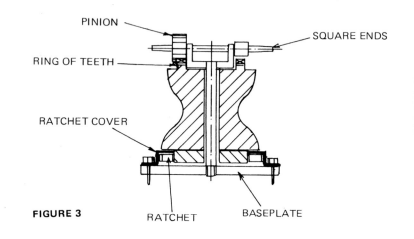

FIGURE 3

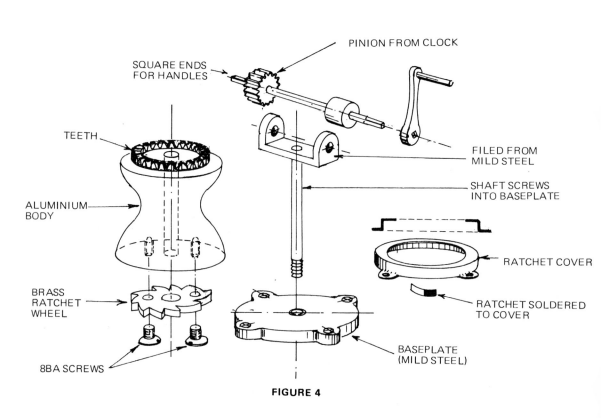

FIGURE 4

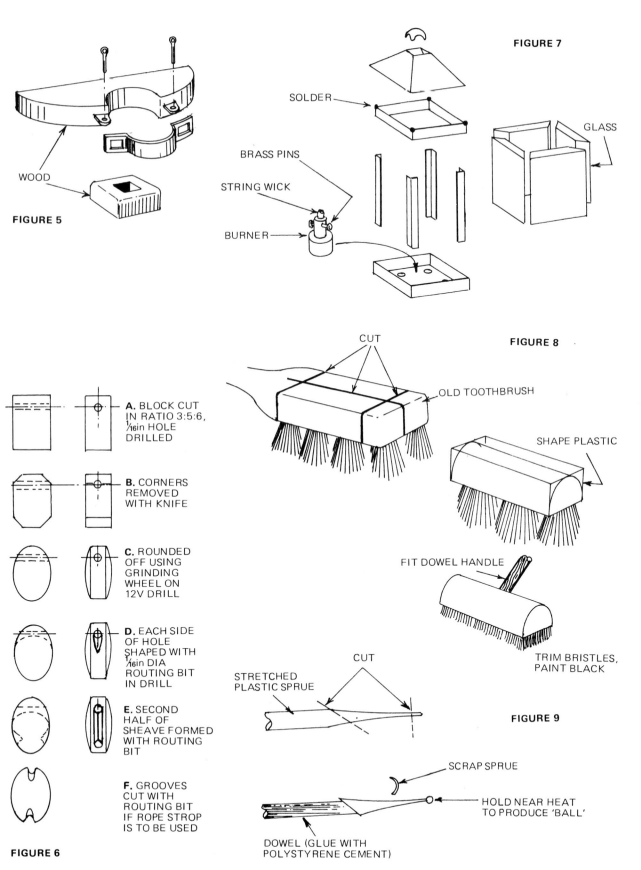

FIGURE 5

WOOD

FIGURE 7

SOLDER

BRASS PINS

STRING WICK

BURNER

GLASS

FIGURE 8

CUT

OLD TOOTHBRUSH

SHAPE PLASTIC

FIT DOWEL HANDLE

TRIM BRISTLES,
PAINT BLACK

A. BLOCK CUT IN RATIO 3:5:6, 1⁄16in HOLE DRILLED

B. CORNERS REMOVED WITH KNIFE

C. ROUNDED OFF USING GRINDING WHEEL ON 12V DRILL

D. EACH SIDE OF HOLE SHAPED WITH 1⁄16in DIA ROUTING BIT IN DRILL

E. SECOND HALF OF SHEAVE FORMED WITH ROUTING BIT

F. GROOVES CUT WITH ROUTING BIT IF ROPE STROP IS TO BE USED

FIGURE 6

CUT

STRETCHED PLASTIC SPRUE

FIGURE 9

SCRAP SPRUE

HOLD NEAR HEAT TO PRODUCE 'BALL'

DOWEL (GLUE WITH POLYSTYRENE CEMENT)

Top: deck planking for the *Industry* model has caulking of black cartridge paper and treenails to simulate stopped holes. Note foremast tabernacle supported by three knees and two feathers. Capstan is turned aluminium – and works!
John Bowen
Centre: another view of the hull, showing the 'busy' overall appearance of the model. The helmsman is carved from cherry and balsa; note the boat's lantern to his right.
John Bowen
Bottom: the hold, with stones overlaying the lead ballasting.
John Bowen

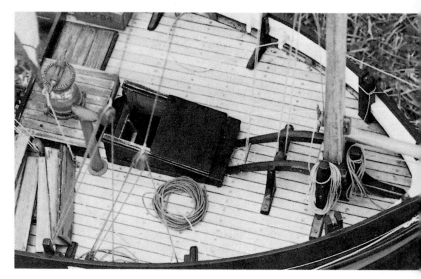

or black. This gave the wood a weathered, slightly dirty appearance. A further coat of clear varnish, followed by a final matt coat, completed the job.

RIGGING, LANTERN AND MISCELLANY

The rigging of the *Industry* was comparatively simple, neither mast being fixed. The foremast fits into a tabernacle and the mizzen steps on the deck, supported by a metal bracket on a wooden block on the transom – see Figure 5. The bowsprit and outrigger are also removable, each fitting into metal brackets.

Figure 6 shows the method I use for making wooden blocks. The wood used is cherry, which I find works well, does not crack and has a suitable colour. Dirty matt varnish can be used to make the colour even deeper if necessary.

One interesting feature shown in photographs of Hastings luggers is the large lantern attached to the mizzenmast 6 or 7ft above the deck. I made this (Figure 7) out of sheet brass, with glass cut from microscope slides. The base was made first, from sheet brass with the sides turned up. The burner unit was made from two short pieces of tube, a smaller top section flattened around the wick (charred string) and fitting into the lower section. Brass pins completed the unit. This was soldered to the centre of the base and the angled corner pieces and top strip of brass added to complete the main frame of the lantern. The four panes of glass slid in at this stage. Each pane had been cut to size and then the

Left: deck details aft. Ballast for trimming is cunningly disguised as a pair of fish-boxes. *John Bowen*

side edges bevelled so that the four panes fitted tightly together inside the lantern. The pyramid-shaped brass top was carefully joined to the rest of the lantern using a single touch of solder at each corner. A small cap, with vent holes, fixed to the top completed the lantern. The finished article when cleaned and polished looked good and was well worth the trouble taken.

At this stage the basic model was complete but the addition of bits and pieces lying around the deck was needed to give it an authentic air. I made an iron stocked anchor, a bucket from sheet brass, several fish-boxes, a broom from part of a toothbrush (Figure 8) and a boat hook (Figure 9).

Hastings luggers carried their oars and spars slung over the port side in raft ropes. I made four oars and a second foreyard and stowed them in that manner. All that was needed then was the helmsman and the ballast.

The helmsman's arms, head and boots were carved from cherry (which takes details well) and the torso and thighs were from balsa. The clothes were made from cloth glued directly on to the figure. The tops of the boots (turned down) were from notepaper, as was the apron and sou'wester. A pipe carved from lignum vitae completed the figure.

The *Industry* carried stones as ballast. I cast two large pieces of lead to fit into the hold, one on either side of the keelson with a flat, level upper surface. A sprinkling of very small stones from the beach covered the lead and gave the correct appearance. The trim of the model showed that it needed a few more ounces of lead in the stern. To rectify this I cast two blocks of lead, each of which fitted into a fish-box. Coils of spare rope were glued on top of the lead, covering it over. These boxes sat neatly in the lute stern behind the transom and gave the correct trim to the model (see Figure 10).

SAILING THE *INDUSTRY*

The model sailed well with no false keel and only a scale rudder. The one problem with a lug rig occurs if the boat inadvertently goes about: the foresail is set aback and the model

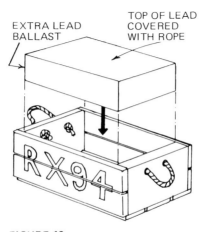

EXTRA LEAD BALLAST

TOP OF LEAD COVERED WITH ROPE

RX94

FIGURE 10

makes little or no progress. Fortunately the *Industry* had both fore and mizzen staysails which if set sufficiently free would, along with the mizzen and mizzen topsail, still produce some power if the model tacked. Together they were able to overcome the pressure on the foresail and gave the model a chance of progressing to the pond side somewhere. When sailing correctly with all five sails drawing well the model looked very realistic, the powerful rig dragging the bluff, heavy hull through the water with a deep bow wave. Her sailing days were few, however, as she was wanted by the Bembridge Maritime Museum, Isle of Wight, as soon as I would part with her. (For some reason, Alan Tulloch, one of the owners of that museum, does not share my enthusiasm for having his exhibits ploughing through the waves!) The model is now on permanent display at Bembridge.

ACKNOWLEDGEMENTS

I should like to thank John Bowen for the loan of his copy of *The Fishing Luggers of Hastings,* Parts I & II, by James Hornell (1938). This book, now sadly out of print, is a wealth of information, particularly with regard to the rigging. Each spar, sail and rope is described in detail, even down to every belaying point. The book proved invaluable.

I should also like to express my thanks to Mr J Burton who kindly opened the Fisherman's Museum in the church of Roc-an-Nore, Hastings. I was able to visit the museum in mid-winter and have a good look at the full-sized lugger *Enterprise* on display in the church. In this small gem of a museum are many interesting photographs, including a stern view of the *Industry* showing all the lettering. There are also several good models and various historic pieces of equipment. I would recommend anyone on holiday in Hastings during the summer months to pay a visit to the church.

THE GREEK PADDLE FRIGATE
EPICHEIRESIS

by Steve Kirby

Above: *Epicheiresis* makes an impressive picture when afloat. This shows well the somewhat unusual shape of the topsides of the hull.

This story begins a long time ago with the Turkish occupation of Greece.

Although there were many minor rebellions from time to time, there was no organised attempt at independence until 1822. For the next two years the rebellion waxed and waned and rapidly developed into a series of scattered skirmishes around the islands. With the threat of the Egyptians joining in on the Turkish side, the Greek rebel leaders sought outside assistance. In 1825 Prince Alexander Mavrocordatos, Secretary of the Greek National Assembly, sent an official invitation to Lord Thomas Cochrane (an English mercenary Admiral) to command the Greek Navy in the continuing war of independence. Cochrane tentatively accepted to lead the Greek rebellion at sea. The Greek Navy was being led by Admiral Miaoulis who, although having achieved much, was beginning to fail, due to the Egyptians joining in on the Turkish side.

Cochrane needed a decent fleet with which to fight, and was given a

free hand to purchase suitable ships, and enough money with which to pay for them. In his renowned pioneering manner he ordered six steamships from England and two large frigates from the USA. The American style frigates suited his plans perfectly, and the latest thing in warships — the steam paddle gunboat — might just provide an overriding advantage. There were long delays over the production of the machinery for the steamers, and the builders of the two frigates in New York got greedy and demanded £200,000 for each ship instead of the contract price of £150,000 for the pair! Furthermore, rumours were rife that the builder of the steamships in London had been bribed by the Turks to delay construction. In April 1826 Admiral Cochrane inspected the steamers under construction and found *Perseverence* (later named *Karteria*) to be nearing completion. *Enterprise* (later named *Epicheiresis*) and *Irrestible* were only two weeks behind, with the remaining three, *Mercury*, *Alert*, and *Dasher* a further

two weeks behind that. In September 1826 (note the five month delay) *Karteria* finally arrived in Greece and offered invaluable service during the last years of the war. Her party piece, apparently, was to set the paddles

Top: the model under way, and showing the hull decoration to advantage.
Below: forecastle showing fitting of the bowsprit and detail at the foot of the foremast.

rotating in opposite directions and spin on her own axis, firing her guns as they came to bear!

Subterfuge, incompetence and 'technical problems' caused enormous delays to the other ships. *Irrestible* sank on trials as the result of a boiler explosion and *Epicheiresis* (nee *Enterprise*) proved, like the others, to be very unreliable and rather unseaworthy. She finally arrived in Greece late in August 1827 (nearly a year after *Karteria*) under the command of Captain Crosby. *Mercury* (renamed *Hermes* by the Greeks) arrived in October 1828, some two years late! *Alert* and *Dasher* were never completed.

Karteria was a flat-bottomed, 4-masted square-rigged vessel with decorative head rails and false stern gallery, intended presumably to make her resemble a frigate. With an 84hp steam engine on each paddle, she made a respectable six knots. *Epicheiresis* and *Irrestible* were completely different in design, being roughly double ended with a 3-masted schooner rig without square sails, but again flat bottomed. Being of much less displacement than *Karteria* two 50hp engines sufficed to achieve the same speed.

The armament of these ships is quoted differently for each source consulted. The Greek Ministry of National Defence — who provided much information for this project — quote *Karteria*'s armament as four 68pdr cannon *and* four 68pdr carronades. This is really rather excessive for a ship of this size. Worse still is that they quote the same for the much lighter *Epicheiresis* and she has only four gunports! Consultation with books and experts came up with the most likely armament of four 32pdr cannon or carronades. I decided to mount four 32pdr cannons on the model, and although this still results in a rather crowded gun deck, I am told that it looks 'about right'.

THE MODEL
I decided to build the model to a scale of ¼in = 1ft (1/48). I reckoned that this would give me a displacement of about 9lb.

Drawings for *Enterprise* are held by the National Maritime Museum at Greenwich and show, very unusually, the ship complete with masts, sails,

rigging and sea! The drawings look impressively complete, but a long close study revealed many inconsistencies, errors and draughting faults, most not becoming apparent until the relevant part of the model had been made.

THE HULL
The basic structure is exactly double-ended, but the design of the upperworks relieves this effect considerably. The angular rakish style is extraordinarily out of keeping with

the solid, rounded elegant lines so well established by this time. The paddles are set well forward in curious angular paddle-boxes which are built up to provide extra accommodation space. Another striking feature is the side decoration in the form of a stylised sea-serpent with its scaly tail starting at the tip of the beak under the bowsprit. A criss-cross patterned body runs the full length of the hull and a fearsome head is turned to look forward from the stern.

Armament comprises four 32pdr cannon on carriages. This does not sound much, but it must be borne in mind that the boilers and machinery would have taken up a great deal of space and would have been heavy for the power produced.

The paddle wheels are very small and carry eight fixed floats each — feathering floats not being in general use at the time.

CONSTRUCTION

The design of the hull, having an overhanging board all round, lent itself to my usual technique of making the whole top half of the model removable for access to the interior.

The hull, being flat-bottomed and slab-sided, was very simple to build using a flat ply base, balsa frames and $\frac{1}{16}$ in ply sides. The resulting hull looked more like a window box than anything else! It was fitted with a false deck with the proper deck and bulwarks built up on top, but without actually being glued to it. This method ensures a good fit and perfect alignment of the 'top-half' of the model. The deck was planked with bass, the caulking being simulated with a black laundry marker. The planks at the deck edge nearly follow the curve of the ship's side, the others gradually becoming straighter until the plank on the centre-line is straight and parallel. This means that virtually every plank has to be curved

and tapered. This happens to be the first planked deck that I have done: what a one to pick!

The gratings on the deck are the only commercial items used on the whole model. Experiments showed that to match the commercial ones for neatness and accuracy was very difficult. The items bought are not assembled as intended because on a full-size grating the top bars are only square section timber resting in the bottom 'comb' cut pieces. If you follow this practice on the model you will not only end up with more accurate gratings but the commercial product will yield twice as much for your money. You will of course need to make the square bars yourself — much easier than making the comb pieces. Finally on gratings, do not forget that they are rarely flat. In fact their curvature is usually greater than that of the deck camber. The exceptions are those gratings which are intended to be stood upon, and these will indeed be flat.

MASTING & RIGGING

I consulted several experts on this subject, perhaps hoping to find an excuse for abandoning the model, but all I got was encouragement and an assurance that the project was valid. This all came about because the odd fittings and decidely strange runs of rigging depicted on the drawing were beginning to put me off the whole thing. However the

main advice which I received was to adopt the general layout of the rigging and sails, plus the spar dimensions shown, but to rig the vessel in accordance with the standard practice of the period, and not always as shown on the rather stylised drawing.

Fortunately there are many books covering this period. By taking bits from here and there I was able to rig the vessel reasonably satisfactorily, bearing in mind the unusual layout and shape of the ship. Everything has been done 'in period', with nothing invented, nevertheless the resulting set-up must be considered somewhat conjectural.

The blocks and deadeyes were made on a small lathe from walnut or boxwood depending on size, but the very small ones were made of brass. The chainplates are all keyed to the outside of the hull, no external chain wales being fitted. Those for the fore and mizen mast pass through the bulwarks to narrow chain wales with belaying pins inboard. The top ends of the chain plates carry the lower deadeyes and blocks for backstays and topmast shrouds. The masts all stand in tabernacles, probably not because the rig was intended to be lowered regularly but to enable the builders to step and raise the masts without using a crane, and to allow battle damage to be dealt with easily where there were no dockyard facilities. The mainmast stays and

shrouds have the upper third made in chain in order to resist the deleterious effects of smoke and embers issuing from the adjacent funnel.

Each mast carries a housing topmast steadied by backstays, forestays, and shrouds. Each topmast carries a topsail, gaff-rigged on the foremast and lug-rigged on the main and mizen masts. At the bow the bowsprit carried inner, outer and flying jibs. This may not seem much to those who model square-rigged ships, but this being the first large, rigged ship that I have made, I was amazed at how long it all took. So much has been written about rigging that I do not need to go into detail. 780 knots for the ratlines represented my first milestone, and making 100 belaying pins did not do much for my sense of humour either. I dare not count the blocks, suffice to say that I made these in four or five sizes as I needed them.

One of the most difficult bits not covered in any books I could find was to work out what happens to all that running rigging when sails are unbent or furled. Some of it is removed complete with the sails, but most of it stays put with the loose ends either shackled together, or fished to the nearest convenient spar or piece of standing rigging. Some sails, usually the smaller ones, are easily removeable along with their running rigging, whereas the larger and heavier courses are left in place and furled when not in use. I have modelled the vessel with topsails and jibs struck, but with courses furled. The topsail yards are shown hoisted to their working positions, mainly to reset the signal halliards which would still be needed when proceeding under steam only.

All running rigging is belayed in approximately the traditional places. The coils of rope are simulated by preformed items hung over the belaying pins after all the rigging had been completed. This preforming is necessary because the cord used on a model is comparatively stiff, and needs to be wound around two pins set in different faces of a plastic block and set with varnish prior to fitting.

PADDLE WHEELS

These are shown on the drawing as having eight fixed floats on each, but otherwise no constructional details are given. I carried out some research into paddle wheel construction of this period, finding the models in the Science Museum particularly useful. All the full-size paddlers around now, including *Reliant* in The National Maritime Museum, have feathering paddles, quite unsuitable for both date and type.

I have seen many models with the paddle wheel rings and spokes fretted from one sheet of metal. Were this practice adopted for the prototype the builder would need several 20ft square sheets of iron to start with! The full-size rings were built up of at least four sectors with separate spokes. I made the rings in one piece for the model, but added small pieces inside to simulate the buttstraps that join the sectors. The spokes are, of course, separate items, the whole lot being soldered up to a turned boss. Two such side plates are required for each wheel, and when aligned in pairs have diagonal cross bracing added in between. The wooden paddle blades, or floats, were almost always held in place by U or J bolts secured with square nuts (hexagonal nuts were not in general use in this period). I used wire U-bolts with dummy nuts, soldered rather than threading them all. However, the completed U-bolt and nut assemblies really do hold the floats to the frame. On each wheel there are 2 rings, 16 spokes, 8 floats, 32 U-bolts, 64 nuts plus buttstraps, diagonal braces, hubs, etc, totalling 142 pieces per wheel in all. All joints, buttstraps, etc received my usual dummy rivet treatment using PVA glue and hypodermic syringe. When painted, the wheels looked quite impressive. I have described this in some detail because so many otherwise fine models of paddlers have been let down by oversimplified and badly made paddle wheels.

GUNS

These are 32pdr smoothbore carriage mounted cannons. The first barrel I made was of brass and looked good, but it was heavy and took a long time to make. Rather than scrap it and make four in perspex, I decided to use it as a master for a silicon-rubber mould, and from this I produced four resin barrels at a fraction of the weight, cost and time.

The carriages were made from plastruct sheet, all eight brackets (the side pieces) being milled out together on a lathe. The axle beams and cross members were made individually and the whole carriage glued together. The trucks (wheels) were turned from perspex rod, and all the ring bolts and fittings are copper wire and brass.

The gun tackles are of standard type rigging blocks and cord, but a very heavy gauge cord was used for the breeching. The gun tools, ie the sponge, rammer, ladle and worm, were made of polystyrene rod with wood, metal and plastic end fittings. The double helix worm was the most difficult. The sponge was simply a rod with a piece of dowel glued on the end (like the rammer), but then wetted with varnish and dipped in model railway scenic light grey flock. This produced a nice sponge which, even if a bit overdone, looks the part. There seems to have been several methods of stowing these sets of tools at each gun. In the absence of any other information, I chose the multi-level system, which looks neat and displays the tools nicely. During my researches I found very few models which had any gun tools to hand. Rows of cannon, piles of shot, open gunports, but not a loading tool in sight. A most curious omission on the part of modelmakers.

BOATS

These were made using the method which I developed initially for producing small boats at small scales — around 1/96 or smaller. So I looked forward to seeing how it would work on a 1/48 scale boat 7in long. Briefly, the process is as follows:

1. Make a solid balsa hull to the shape required but about 0.040in undersize on the beam. Attach a handle about 3in long, 1½in wide made of ¼in balsa to the flat top of the solid hull. This is the plug.
2. Make a ⅛in ply plate 2in longer

and wider than the hull with a hole in it to take the plug, leaving a 0.020in gap clearance all round.

3. Clip or peg a piece of 0.015in or 0.020in plasticard (not plastruct) to the ply plate and heat in front of a fire or under a grill. When the plastic becomes soft and droopy (and may even smoke a little) press the balsa plug into the hole carrying the hot plastic with it. Hold for a few seconds to cool.

4. The resulting light shell can now be trimmed to size and fitted out with timbers, inwales, floors, thwarts, etc internally, and with clinker planking, rubbing strips, keel, etc on the outside. It is a fiddly but worthwhile process.

The two boats on the ship are essentially the same, one being a 'bay' shorter than the other. I made two long shells from the same mould, one having a piece cut out for the shorter boat.

Opposite top: the after end of the starboard sponson. Note the hammock stowage.
Opposite bottom: this gives a good idea of the detail put into the ship's boats. Note the ship's wheel abaft the mizzen mast.

Below: close up of the decoration on the stern. Despite the residue from the model's last 'voyage' this shows also the details of the rudder and its fittings.
All photographs by the author.

DETAILS

Most of the detail work is fairly straightforward but one item that creates much interest is the carved 'frieze'. This was done by making moulds for the different shapes involved. No patterns were used, the moulds being produced by engraving directly into a thick plastic sheet rather like an intaglio carving.

A hard plastic scraper was used to wipe car body filler into the recesses, and when nearly cured the resulting mouldings were peeled out carefully and laid on a flat surface to be painted. They were then stuck in place, still before being fully cured, so that they would take up the curves of the hull before the material set hard and became brittle. I made the two different criss-cross designs and one scaly tail design moulds which would serve for both sides, and a handed pair of heads for the stern quarters. This made a total of five moulds measuring 35in to produce over 7ft of mouldings for the model. The cabin doors were made roughly the same way, one mould sufficing for all six doors. The door mould was built up with strips of plasticard with the required decoration being engraved into the centre panels.

PROBLEMS ON THE WATER

On my last four models in a row the rudders proved to be quite ineffective. In two cases this was because the rudders were ahead of the propellers and on the other two the rudders were just inexplicably quite useless. Added to this experience I had seen many paddlers needing rudders the size of dining room tables to make them turn. So I decided to do my usual, that is, to propel and steer using only the propellers, or in this instance the paddles. The rudder would simply be attached as a non-working appendage. As it happens the original ship had separate engines to each paddle, so to do the same on the model would not be cheating. Great was my disappointment therefore to find that when in the water the model went ahead and astern rapidly on command, but was not at all keen

to turn, even with paddles rotating furiously in opposite directions. So the rudder was rehung on gudgeons and pintles and connected to a servo using thin flat brass strips. This was necessary due to the confined space in the pointed stern. The model now steers very well, despite the small size of this (scale) rudder.

DATA

The main particulars of *Epicheiresis* are:

Contracted – 1825
Launched – March 1826
Delivered – August 1827
Decommissioned – 1830
Builder – Daniel Brent, Rotherhithe, London
Length – 150ft between perpendiculars
Breadth – 26ft
Displacement – 450 tons burthen
Machinery – Two sets 50hp steam engines
Speed – 6 knots
Consumption – 9 tons of coal per day
Armament – 4 x 32pdr cannon

PLANS

Drawings of *Enterprise* in the National Maritime Museum, Greenwich, London Nos T-12006 and T-12006A

BOOKS CONSULTED

The Masting and Rigging of English Ships of War 1625-1860 by James Lees. *Modelling the Brig of War Irene* by E W Petrejus. *Masting & Rigging*, *The Clipper Ship* and *Ocean Carrier* by Harold A Underhill. *The Anatomy of Nelson's Ships* by C Nepean Longridge. *Cochrane* by Donald Thomas.

ACKNOWLEDGEMENTS

I would like to record my appreciation of the help which I received for this project from the Hellenic Navy Command in Athens, and from the Public Relations Office of the Hellenic Navy General Staff, Ministry of National Defence, Athens in the way of contacts and historical information. To Mr David White my thanks for invaluable technical advice.

THE WHALING BRIGANTINE
VIOLA

by Lloyd McCaffery

In choosing a ship as a subject for a miniature, one of the major factors I consider is the overall appearance of the vessel. By this I mean her aesthetic qualities, the shape and proportions of the hull and rig — in short, whether or not she is an attractive craft from the visual point of view. I am attracted to ships in general, and certain ones in particular mainly because of their good looks. The historical significance is a factor, of course, and it is a happy coincidence when a ship has both good looks and is important because of some event or activity.

Viola is just such a vessel. To my eye she is the most attractive of all the whaleships to which we have access through archival records. She has fine, sweet lines, a lovely clipper bow, and a transom that they call a goose's ass stern up in Gloucester, Massachusetts. Her marked sheer, running up forward in a sweeping line to her single stick bowsprit, makes her as fine a picture of a ship as you could want. The fascinating and intricate deck gear associated with whaling further enhances her qualities.

Historically she is interesting as one of the last ships built for whaling, being launched in 1910. She is not exactly representative of the large number of brigs and brigantines built for this purpose, since she appears to have a much finer model in her lines than was usual. So much the better for us, as she looks like a

clipper, or even a yacht. In fact there is a story going around that she was designed as a yacht and later converted to whaling. This is not true, although we can see readily how this idea could have originated.

Viola was built at Essex, Massachusetts, for Captain John A Cook. He wrote in a book on his career in whaling, *Pursuing the Whale*, regarding the birth of the vessel, and I quote from page 338:

> Feeling that the continued warmth of the tropical climate for a couple of years might benefit Mrs Cook, I entered into a contract with Tarr and James, of Essex, Massachusetts to construct and equip me a brigantine for

sperm whaling. In November 1909 the keel was laid. June 1, 1910 the vessel, named *Viola* for Mrs Cook, was launched.

Viola sailed on 29 June 1910 on her first voyage. She worked the whaling grounds in the North Atlantic in the summer, and was off the west coast of Africa in the winter. On this first voyage she took one hundred and fifty pounds of ambergris, which later sold in New York for $30,000. Her take of oil totalled 2151 barrels.

She made a total of four voyages with Cook as owner and agent, tbough he was not always her captain. On the third voyage he had motion pictures taken on board showing the full sequence of the actual operation of whaling. Several museums in the New England area have copies of this film, but I have been unable to

obtain a copy of my own. I hope that the reclusive attitudes which unfortunately characterise these institutions at times will be rectified and that the film will be made more generally available.

In September 1918 she sailed with Captain Joseph Lewis, his wife and five-year-old daughter, and twenty four crewmen. She was never heard from again after leaving port. As Captain Cook writes (again in *Pursuing the Whale*):

> Lost in the mysteries of the sea with all hands. Sad the fate that has befallen so many that have pursued the sea in ships.

SOURCES OF INFORMATION

My basic source of information on this ship was the set of plans drawn

Below: a good view under the transom as *Viola* was being built on the ways. Note that she was registered at Portland, Maine: this was changed later to New Bedford, Massachusetts.
Photograph: courtesy of the Peabody Museum of Salem, Massachusetts.

up by Walter Channing of Marion, Massachusetts. These consist of two sheets, one showing hull lines and deck details, the other the rigging plan. They are based on the original drawings of the vessel by her designer, William T Adams of East Boothbay, Maine. Mr Erik Ronnberg Jr, of Rockport, Mass. who is an authority on these vessels and much else besides, showed me a tracing made from these plans by, I believe, Howard Chapelle. It was evident that some refairing was needed to make them work out right, and I incorporated these corrections when making the hull. It has been said that there is not a single commercially available plan that does not have some errors or require some alterations — this is why I try always to work from primary source material if at all possible. With the remarkable photographs which are available of *Viola* I was able to make whatever corrections were necessary, as well as to give better definition to some of the deck gear. These photographs came from the Peabody Museum, Salem, Massachusetts, and from the New Bedford Whaling Museum, New Bedford, Massachusetts. They are excellent for their sharpness and wealth of detail. The books shown in the bibliography also contain some good photographs of *Viola*.

CONSTRUCTION
The construction of *Viola* was basically the same as that for the *L A Dunton* (*Model Shipwright* 44).

Top: port side, showing how the painted rail separates the natural-finished planking from the interior painted deck fittings.
Centre: broadside of the model as mounted on the base. She has a very sleek, yacht-like appearance.
Bottom: an area with a lot of detail and interest in the tryworks and carpenter's bench.
Opposite top: starboard side: each copper plate was cut from shim stock.
Opposite centre: detail of the cutting in area, with crew members engaged in various activities. Several make scrimshaw, while one is building a model of the *Viola*. Only the cooper, banging away at his bench, seems to be sticking to his job.
Opposite bottom: the model seen from the starboard side, giving a good idea of the general layout of the deck.

All uncredited photographs by the author.

The frames were built up with 1/28in maple veneer, the hull form being shaped out of a block of these veneer pieces. This block was then taken apart, hollowed out, and the spacing pieces between each frame removed. The keel, stem and sternpost were fitted together using the appropriate scarph joints. All these joints were cut with an ordinary single-edge razor blade. Incidentally, I see, and have seen, many plank-on-frame models built with the keel in a single piece. This is not correct, for it means that the original piece would have been some eighty or more feet long! I suspect that many of these models have been built simply as shown on the plans, thus perpetuating the errors already in those plans. It pays to ask yourself some critical questions about the plans you intend to use. Again, try to locate the original source material and use it. We have ready access to a tremendous body of knowledge concerning ships, but few seem to avail themselves of it. Research does take time, but it is essential if the results of your labor are to be worthwhile.

The starboard side was painted and coppered to represent the vessel as she would actually appear. This required some careful thought as to the method of planking. I wanted the seams of the plank to show even though the planks were painted. So, very carefully, I put a rounded edge on the planks by scraping and sanding. When fitted to the hull the resulting V-shaped groove between the planks showed a highlight and shadow on the respective edges, looking just like the side of the ship as seen in the photographs.

It is small touches like this which bring a model to life. The builder must develop an aesthetic awareness, consider the visual impact the finished product will have, and learn to compose the model as a work of art. The important thing is the overall effect the whole creation will have on the viewer.

Consider the matter just presented, defining the edges of the planking. By changing the direction and intensity of the light sources, details can be washed out or be brought into sharp focus. By using just such a subtle technique as creating highlight and shadow on the planks light can

be used as a tool in the presentation of the work. This is another reason why I mount my work on a mirror. Basically, of course, this is to allow the details of the underbody to be seen. However the mirror acts also as a secondary light source, collecting overhead light and throwing it up on the underside of the hull, thus highlighting the work and further defining the shape and form. Since it is lit from several sources dark shadows are eliminated and the viewer can see all the details.

The deck was built up out of holly. I cut the planks from several different billets, being careful to use pieces that vary in colour and value. These are arranged carefully in what appears as a random design on the deck. The juxtaposition of these planks adds interest. The addition of deck gear, crew, etc, makes an overlay of detail and adds texture.

The copper sheathing on the bottom was cut on the lathe, but not in the usual way a lathe is used. I glued a sheet of copper to the top of the table saw attachment of my Unimat. With a straightedge anchored firmly over this table I could advance the tool rest, which held the table, by the desired amount and cut each line of plates. In this way they can be cut to a tolerance of 0.001 in. This is a great help at small scales, as each plate is just over $\frac{1}{16}$ in x $\frac{1}{4}$ in in size.

FIGURES
Few of the figures which I have seen on contemporary models have been high artistic quality. I doubt if many builders have, or have had, the advantage of an artistic background or training. If anyone can take a foundation course in basic drawing, life drawing, two- or three-dimensional design, and composition I would strongly recommend so doing. Learn about anatomy, proportions, and how to capture the gesture of the human form, ie, what the figure is doing — the essence of the pose. Such knowledge of course, can be applied directly to the carving of decorations on the ship itself.

I use a wire armature for my figures, at least the ones at $\frac{1}{16}$ in scale. The large figureheads are carved from solid wood or built up of wax or plasticine. I work out carefully the flow and rhythm of the figure, and plan ahead as to what each will be doing when placed on the work. I design these figures into clusters of activity that add interest to certain areas of the work. They should not exist simply to occupy time and space, but be engaged in some definite activity.

COMPLETION
I will not address all the different aspects involved in the creation of *Viola* here, but just mention one or two more points that I consider important. I mount the vessel on two pedestals built up out of wood and brass and finished with gold leaf. This finish ties in with that of the nameplate and helps to unite these elements of the composition. The pedestals are slotted to receive the keel. This assembly is drilled through athwartships and a brass pin is driven through the keel and the pedestal. The pedestals, with model mounted on them, are epoxied to the mirror. In this way the whole work is firmly anchored.

The glass case is held together with clear silicone sealant. I do not know if readers outside America have access to such a product, but for me it provides a permanent and stable adhesive. The seams of the glass are covered with L-section brass strips.

As a part of this whole package I did several drawings of *Viola*, and a piece of scrimshaw. The latter is a flat piece of ivory with the lines of *Viola* engraved thereon. These pieces were placed in a drawer in the base of the model's case. The result is a self-contained collection in miniature with all the elements related to *Viola*.

The work was consigned to the Mystic Seaport Museum Store Gallery, and the collector who acquired it has generously allowed it to remain on display at the gallery for a period.

BIBLIOGRAPHY
Church, Albert Cook *Whale Ships and Whaling*. W W Norton, 1938.
Cook, John *Pursuing the Whale*.
The American Neptune Pictorial Supplement XV, Photographs of Whaling Vessels. Peabody Museum of Salem, Massachusetts, 1973.

HMS Anson

by J J Taylor

Navy Board models have been a feature of a number of articles in *Model Shipwright* over the years. These models represent a style of construction that must have been popular both with naval authorities of the day and with contemporary modelmakers. I have no intention of describing the method of construction for it is well known. Instead I will tell of some of the planning that went into my Navy Board style model of the *Anson*, of the timber used, and of the snags and errors. The photographs will, I hope, illustrate much of the work carried out.

Anson was a Fourth Rate of 60 guns, built by Mr Ewer of Burlesdon and launched in 1747. The dimensions were: length of gun deck 150ft 0in, extreme breadth 42ft 8in, depth of hold 18ft 6in.

I decided to work to a scale of 1/48 because hitherto I had done very little

Starboard bow quarter view. The gun deck and the main deck have been completed with all guns in position.

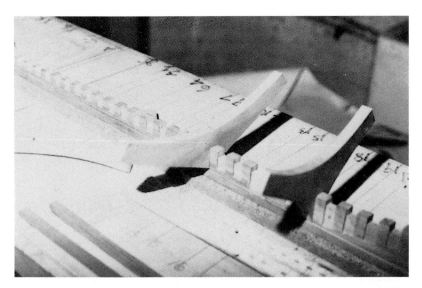

The keel in position on the building board, showing the cut-outs for the floors. The depth of the floor at centre has been increased to give strength across the grain of the wood.

The gun deck has been built up and the pillars are in position. The main deck accommodation is being built up.

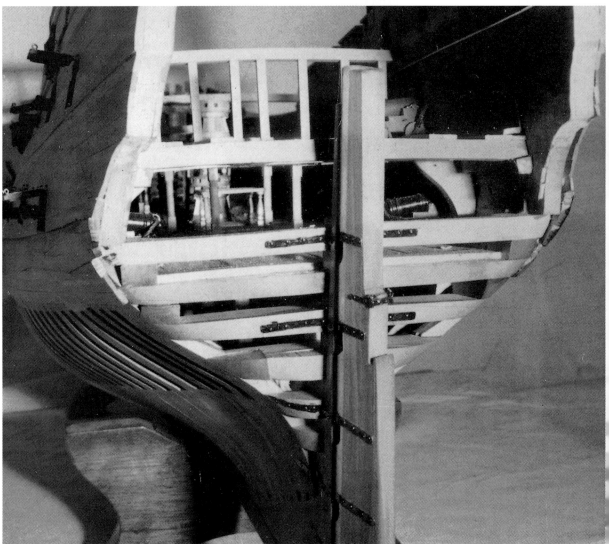

A general view of the stern timbering.

work at this scale. One of the deciding, or limiting factors, had always been – can it be got out of the house, and where will it, with its glass case, be put? The next step was the drawing board. I obtained the draught for the ship from the National Maritime Museum (the reference numbers in the NMM list are 1252/24 to 1256/24, five sheets in all). It was to a scale of 1/96, and consisted of the usual sheer and body plans, with outline plan views of the forecastle head, orlop, gun, upper, quarter and poop decks. These showed little or no detail other than the deck openings, stairways, hatches, gratings, masts and steering position. The main object seems to have been to indicate the positions of the beams. Therefore I had to make a new drawing to 1/48 scale. The first print was used for drawing in the parts of the keel, floors, futtocks, top timbers and filling pieces. On the body plan two bands of timber running from stem to stern were shown, a characteristic of a Navy Board model. When drawing in the main wale I must admit that I modified the line of sheer slightly by dropping the curve amid-

ships by about ⅛in to give the model a little more grace. More time spent on the drawing board at this stage is time well spent, but it can and often does mean a lot of head scratching and rubbing out.

I suppose that there are many different ways of starting to build a ship model. I decided to build on a board; this was 2ft wide by 4ft 6in long, and was given a coat of flat white paint. A centreline was scored down the length of the board, and two more lines were marked on to show the width of the keel. Starting at the middle, the dead flat, the stations were marked and scored across the board at 90° to the centre line, and were numbered and lettered in accordance with the draught.

Two strips of wood about ¼in square were fastened down either side of the keel outline to hold the keel in place along the centreline. The keel itself was built up of three pieces of timber, with two scarph joints, wedged, and the sternpost was fitted. The fore end of the keel ended where the gripe of the stem joined it; there are many varia-

tions of this joint. The stemson was fitted and the rabbet cut in. Supporting brackets were screwed to the baseboard to hold the stem and the sternpost upright, at about 5in above the keel.

The keel was marked out for the slots into which the floors would be fitted. This was the first snag. These had to be very accurately positioned, for the space in between the floors had to be exactly the same as the futtocks which fit in between, thus forming a band of timber each side from stem to stern.

Starting at the stern, the wing transom and the filling transoms were fitted to the fashion pieces, which were slotted into the deadwood on the keel. The floors were marked out from the body plan along with the futtocks. In fitting them in place I found it best to fix one floor and then its futtock, fastening them together in the right place. The next floor was then fastened to the previous futtock, and so on towards the stem. I am not absolutely sure that slotting the deadwood and sinking the

The bow, showing the heads, knightheads, and the main deck under the forecastle deck. Note that the guns are being fastened in place as the building progresses.

chocks, and with the keelson fastened down on top of them.

On reaching the bow, no cant frames were used. The floors were carried on right up to where the cant frames would have been and a solid block was fitted either side of the stem deadwood against the last floor; the hawse pieces sat on this. Of course there are no 'rules' about which way round the hull should be built. It is just a matter of personal choice, and anyway there are 412 pieces to fit together to form the hull whatever the method adopted!

The timber I used was knysna; this is a South African wood similar to Venezuelan boxwood or zapatero as it is sometimes called. It is a creamy coloured wood, varying to greeny brown, and it takes glue very well, though it is slightly abrasive and edge tools need frequent sharpening. The going is easier if lime or pear woods are used.

Having completed the hull framing, the whole structure had to be tied up with the wales. The hull had been shaped and sanded down to conform to the templates, and the position of the wales clearly marked out. It is as well to point out here that their sheer differs from that of the decks, which is why some of the gunports cut into the wales. Anchor stock planking was used. These were 5in in length, and a jig was used to ensure a uniform taper on all the pieces, $\frac{5}{16}$in at the centre to 5/32in at the ends. Starting amidships the planks were laid up, glued, clamped and treenailed into position. Rounding the bow, I carved each piece and fitted them in place, finishing off afterwards to thickness. The height of the bulwarks was marked out next; these were cut down minus the thickness of the plank sheer or cap rail, which was put on after the moulding had been fitted and fastened.

The shell of the hull was now ready for planking, but before starting this I faired off the inside, smoothing down the numerous joints, and put in the mast steps on top of the keelson. These may never be used, but it was little trouble to fit them. The gunports, 32 on each side, were marked out, those on the gun deck being slightly bigger than the others. Care was taken to follow the deck line and not the sheer when doing this. I cut out the gunports with a trepanning drill, removed the corners, and finished the squaring off

floor into it is really the best way. As timber has a tendency to move where there is moisture in the air and with changes in temperature, and as there are hundreds of pieces of varying sizes and shapes in a ship model, it did occur to me that just cutting a slot in the floors and allowing them to sit on top of the keel, thereby allowing some movement to take place without imposing a stress on the parts as they were being assembled, might be a suitable alternative. But whether the floors are allowed to move or not, ultimately they will be held in place by

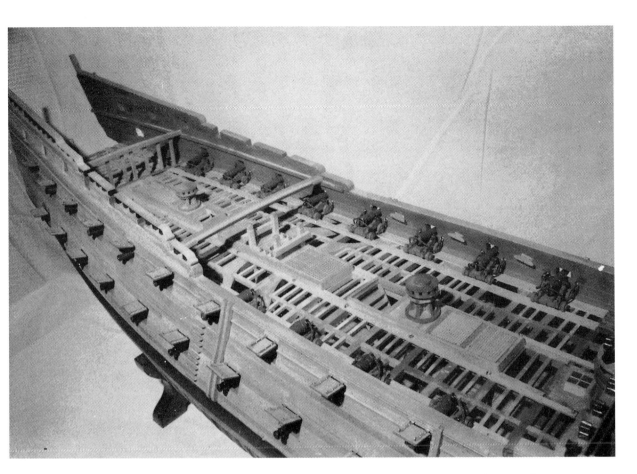

The main deck. The break of the quarter beam is in place on its shelf, and the framework for the partition of the after accommodation has been erected.

The quarter deck beam, showing its face moulding. The after capstan and the mainmast bits have been fitted.

process with a rough square-section file. The ceiling came next, and this was taken from gundeck level to the full height of the poop deck, and was cut off flush at the gunports. Work on the interior continued with fitting the beam shelves. The top edge of the shelf was one deck thickness and one depth of beam below the deck line. Along the beam shelf line a series of 0.020in holes were drilled, and pins were pushed through to form a datum line for the beam shelf. The shelf, $\frac{3}{16}$in square in section and drilled for retaining screws, was offered up to the pins, clamped in place and screwed down.

Starting at the bow, the deck hooks were fastened in place, but the knees and beams were not included since this deck was completely planked over, with only the openings for the gratings, hatches and stairs. The beams were placed on the shelves and fastened. They were placed as shown on the draught, and pillars were fitted between the beams and keelson at regular intervals.

The deck planking was laid from the

The forecastle deck timbering completed, and showing the foremast deck ring and bitts, belfry, galley stove pipe and gratings.

centre, ie the king plank, outwards to the bulwarks, where it met the edge plank. This was overlaid with a waterway board, which also served as a stop for the gun carriage wheels when in the run-out position. Before the deck was completely covered the timber for the bitts was secured to the beams, and the manger built, after which the planking was completed. The gunports were lined, coming flush with the ceilings and flush with the hull, and the insides were painted at this stage, using a matt, not gloss, paint; I used poster colour, which dried dull and even.

The guns were turned from brass in the lathe, using two form cutters. One was for the long barrels, and the other for the short barrels. They can, of course, be made from wood just as well. In this case a heavy lathe was available, also the material. There were 26 24-pdr guns on the gun deck, and all these had

long barrels. The remaining guns were all 24-pdr short barrel ones. These, according to some sources, should be 12-pdrs, but I used 18-pdrs as on the model they looked better. The gun carriages were practically all alike, the only differences being very small. The guns, all 26 of them, were screwed in place, complete with breeching rope with eyes ready to be connected to the eyebolts in the bulwarks. The only other fittings were the gun tackles for drawing the guns inboard; one block was fastened to the rear axle of the carriage and the other to an eyebolt in the deck.

The outside planking was completed, starting at the upper edge of the wale and working upwards, stopping short at the port linings so as to leave a rebate for the gunport lids. Thicker planking was used when the upper wale was reached, after which various mouldings were worked into the lay of the planking. The plank sheer, or capping rail, was fitted, together with the hance pieces.

The head rails of the ship consisted of

four upright timbers and five horizontal ones. The lower cheek bracket started in the middle of the wale almost at the first gunport, forming a knee where it met the knee of the head, and ran out to the main piece just below the figurehead. The upper cheek started above the wale and ran to the underside of the gammoning piece, and rose up behind the figurehead. The hawse hole piece with its bolster sat on the upper cheek rail. The third rail, or ekeing rail, dropped from the cathead knee to the hawse hole piece and continued as the lower rail to the hair bracket formed by the upper cheek. The fourth, or upper, rail, started at the bow and ran parallel to the hair bracket. Finally, the main rail ran from the timber head, forward of the cathead, to the hair bracket. The four upright timbers crossed the third and fourth at various angles, making it very difficult to describe – and more difficult to make. I made four sets of timbers before getting anything like a reasonable result, and I found that making templates came just as hard as making the actual parts! All the outer

faces of the timbers were moulded in the usual manner. The head works were complete with the heads, gratings and false rails. The knightheads, stem, apron and stemson were then finished. The beakhead bulkhead was fitted, along with the roundhouses and mouldings, finishing off with the planksheer. The whole deck was cleaned down and given two coats of synthetic picture varnish, using a spray; it dried matt.

Work now started on the main deck. As on the gun deck the beam shelf was fitted first. A datum line representing the upper edge of the shelf was marked on the inside of both bulwarks, being positioned the depth of the beam plus the thickness of the deck below the line of the deck. This deck included the hanging knees, lodging knees, beam arms, carlings – side and middle tiers – binding strakes, and the ledges. Starting at the forecastle head with the deck hook, the beams were fitted and fastened to the beam shelf, along with the lodging and hanging knees. The deck openings were built as the work

The break of the forecastle, showing the panelled front and moulded head rail with timber heads.

The gun deck at the mainmast, with the main deck beam arms in place. Note the capstan with the socket for the connecting spindle to the main deck capstan.

advanced, and pillars were fitted under the beams in the appropriate places. After the beams had been fitted the hatch, gratings and stairway coamings were fixed, along with capstan platforms and the mast partners. Only planking alongside the coamings was fitted, so as to show as much of the construction as possible.

The forecastle head was built up; the bulkhead, which was panelled, had a bowed centre section which housed the galley stove. Beam shelves were used, and the deck was built up as before, using lodging and hanging knees. Only edge planks were fitted. The cathead beam, which was made in two pieces with a long splice in the centre, was fastened up against the forward bulkhead. The mast partners were fitted with a mast ring, and at the corners the forecastle bitts were fastened to the beams of the upper deck. Between the mast and the belfry there was a grating, and the ventilator with the galley stove pipe rose through it. The belfry dome or cover was carved from the solid, and had a turned pillar at each of the four corners. The bell was

The quarter deck, complete with double steering wheels. Note the channels and the deadeye straps; chain links were not in use at this period.

The steering position under the break of the poop. There is no glass in the partition. Not all ships had a large expanse of glass in this partition since the captain's bed place was just behind the steering position.

The break of the quarter deck, with gratings and ladders fitted. Note the pillars under the beam.

The gun deck before being covered over, showing the after capstan and stairway to the after magazine. The 26 24-pdr long barrel guns are all in position.

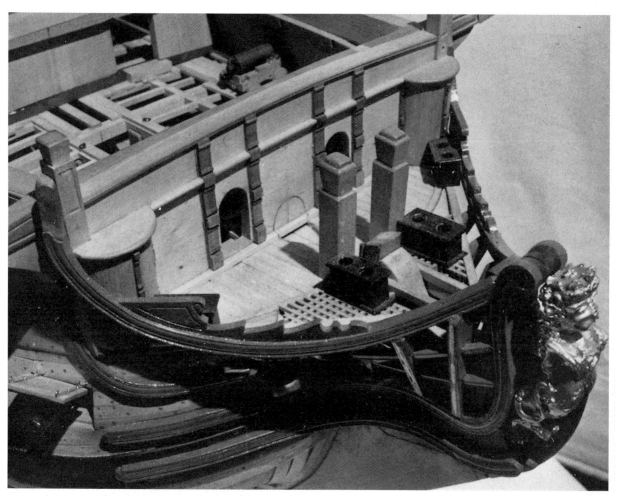

The head of the ship, but not yet completed.

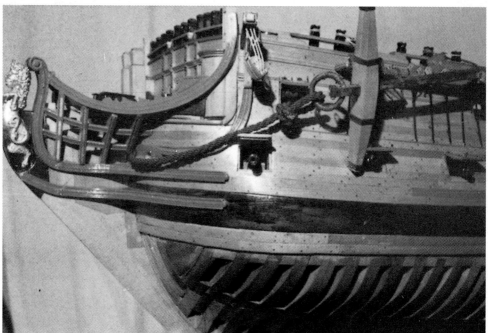

The port bow, showing the rails and anchor stowage.

brass, turned up to the pattern of the time.

The quarter deck was fully beamed with hanging and lodging knees fitted on the beam shelf. This deck was fully planked except for two open spaces between the guns and the gratings, and the stairways extended from just beyond the edge of the quarter deck to the cabin bulkhead. After the stag-horns and kevels had been fitted the guns were screwed down in position. Breech ropes were fitted but no train-ing tackles – only the ring bolts. Under the break of the poop was the steering position with the double wheel. The construction of this double wheel was as follows. Two rims were turned out of lignum vitae, with a slight recess to receive four brass rings. These were fastened in place with rivets, and they served to reinforce the rim while it was being drilled to take the spokes and handles. The turned spokes were fitted into a groove formed at each end of the rope drum, and secured with a brass

boss pad outside the supporting stands. The whole assembly was fitted on to a platform with a grating on each side. Beyond the bulkhead lay the officers' accommodation.

The poop deck was raised at the break in order to provide headroom at the steering position and in the cabins. The deck was planked over, but with spaces left to show the cabin interiors. Three large knees butted up against the taffrail.

The lower counter was built up on timbers fastened to the wing transom. These had to be carefully spaced out to allow the two gunports to be placed on either side of the rudder. The counter was planked from the tuck rail to the lower moulded rail on the upper coun-ter. The upper counter was left plain and painted, with moulded rails top and bottom. A row of five windows was built on the upper counter and one each in the quarter galleries, which were built up under the stern walk. The stern walk had turned pillars to form a

balustrade. At the after end of the quarter galleries were two Roman military figures, connecting the ship with Lord Anson's famous ship *Centurion*. The stern walk bulkhead was panelled, and was fitted with windows and a door. The decoration was simple the usual stands of arms, dolphins, and a badge with the Royal cypher over which was mounted a bust.

I think that the decorative work is a point which puts off many ship modellers from building this type of ship. Even to contemplate copying the carvings and decorative work from a contemporary model is a daunting task. The best substitutes which I have found are in the products for military modellers. There are extensive ranges of figures available, and I have used some of these models which, with a certain amount of reshaping, have pro-duced an effect which is far better than

The lower stern windows and gallery.

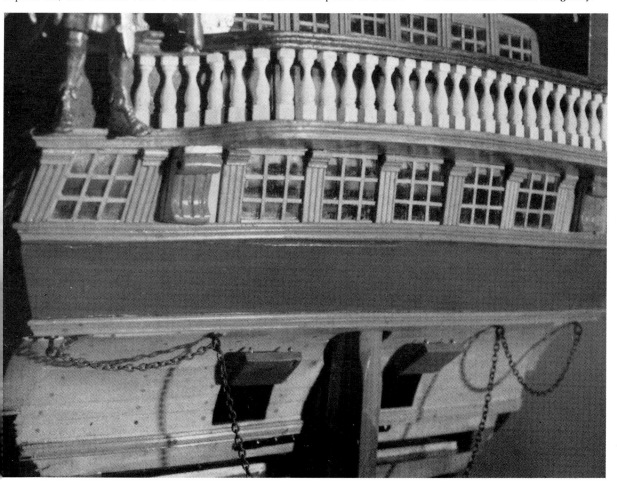

anything which I could hope to achieve. The type of decoration which was present on the *Anson* when she was built is not known, but Romanesque figures seemed to be the fashion at that time. In order to offset the expanse of outside planking, which was relieved only by the channels and their straps, ebony top timbers were used on which were mounted the capping rails.

A set of lanterns was mounted on the stern. Whether these were fitted as an optional extra, adding to the overall decorative effect of the stern, was not quite clear, though they must have had some use as an aid to navigation whilst station keeping at night. It is a little difficult to say which is correct for which period. The three fitted on *Anson* were six-sided with eighteen lights, and tapered.

History

Anson was commissioned in 1747. In 1748 the ship was under the command of the Honourable Augustus Keppel, and joined Warren's fleet. From 1749–1752 she was guard ship at Portsmouth under Captain Justinian Mutt, and again from 1753 to 1754

under Captain Charles Holmes. In 1755, under Captain Robert Mann, she saw service with Boscawen's squadron in North America. 1756 found her in the Leeward Islands. From 1759 to 1763 she was in Hawke's fleet under the command of Captain Matthew Whitwell. In 1760 she was in the Western Squadron, and on 6th September of that year sailed for the Mediterranean. In 1763, whilst still under the command of Captain Whitwell, she was paid off, and was sold later that year.

References

The plans used for the model were Nos 1252/24 to 1256/24 (five sheets in all) in the National Maritime Museum Catalogue or Plan List.
Howard, Frank, *Sailing Ships of War, 1400–1860*
Lavery, Brian, *The Ship of the Line*, Vols I & II
Longridge, C Nepean, *The Anatomy of Nelson's Ships*
Model Shipwright (various issues).

Conclusion

Finally I would like to thank the staff of

the National Maritime Museum and Mr J Roome of the Science Museum for much invaluable assistance. My thanks, too, to Mr T Lancaster for taking the photographs which accompany this article.

The Captain's stern walk. It shows the vulnerability of these ships when attacked from the rear.

All photographs by T Lancaster.

TRADITIONAL

Wooden
Shipbuilding

PART 9
by David White

Flat of the deck

The decks of all ships of 28 guns and above are usually of 3in plank. The wood was deal (fir) or oak, or a combination of both. Plank widths and lengths varied, not only with the type of wood used but also according to its current availability. English oak plank was seldom more than 24ft in length whereas *East Country* or *Dantzic* oak was obtainable in lengths of 30 to 50ft. *Deals* were usually around 36 to 40ft long, and occasionally even longer. (*Deals* was a general term used to describe deal planks.) Oak planks were usually wider than deals, an average figure in the second half of the eighteenth century

being around 8 to 12in for oak and 7 to 10in for deals, although these figures could, and did, vary considerably. In the early years of the eighteenth century oak plank of up to 24in was not uncommon. Ships' decks narrowed towards the ends and the planks followed suit by being tapered, but they were not normally reduced to less than 6in in width.

Fastenings varied according to which deck they were used on, the type of timber used and the period. The number of fastenings depended largely upon the width of the plank but was not as consistent as it is sometimes made out to be. Several publications

give details about numbers and types of deck fastenings, based on the width of the plank. These all appear to have been taken from *Lloyd's Rules for Merchant Ships* of the mid-nineteenth century and have no bearing whatsoever on earlier merchantmen, or warships of any period.

In general it can be said that the oak planking of warships' gundecks tended to have two iron bolts in each beam and one treenail in each ledge. Deal decks, on the other hand, were usually fastened with a couple of iron spikes or nails in the beams and one, or occasionally two, in the ledges. All decks were caulked, with the exception of the orlops and platforms.

Upper deck

At first glance the planking of a ship's deck appears to be quite straightforward but closer inspection reveals it to be quite a complex jigsaw puzzle. Fig 1 shows a typical deck section, through the main hatchway. At the outer end was the *waterway*, which was between 1 and 2ft wide; 'as broad as may be had' or 'as broad as can be gotten' were typical specifications. In ships of 28 guns and upwards, it was usually 2in thicker, at its thickest part, than the flat of the deck; with the exception of some three-deckers where it was 3in thicker. In 24-gun ships it was 1½in thicker; in 18-gun sloops the figure was 1in. As the flat of the deck was 3in thick in all these

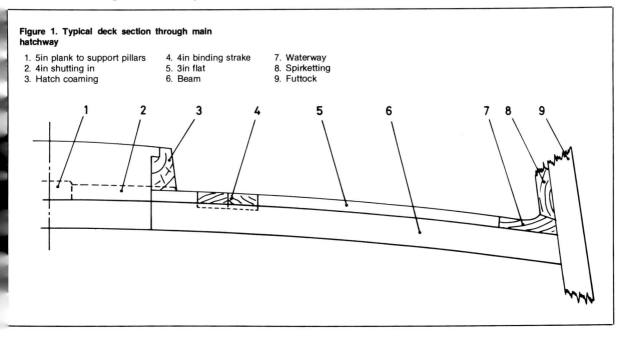

Figure 1. Typical deck section through main hatchway

1. 5in plank to support pillars
2. 4in shutting in
3. Hatch coaming
4. 4in binding strake
5. 3in flat
6. Beam
7. Waterway
8. Spirketting
9. Futtock

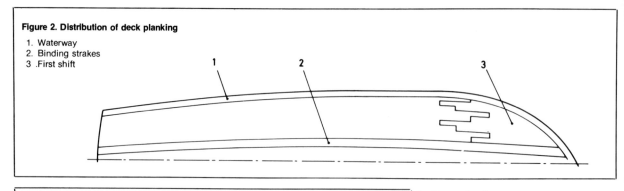

Gun deck

The flat of the gun decks in two- and three-deckers followed the construction of the upper deck in principle but differed in detail. Waterways and binding strakes remained the same but as this deck carried heavier guns than the upper deck, the rest of the flat was usually all oak with the outer strakes worked top and butt, even if the upper deck ones were not.

Between the hatchways etc the shutting in was 1in thicker than the flat, with the outer edges rounded down. Occasionally the midship strake or strakes would be 1in thicker still, to provide a base for the pillars supporting the deck above (fig 1).

It is appropriate at this stage to point out that the *king plank*, which appears in yachts and in the wooden sheathing of some steel-decked ships, did not exist in traditionally built ships; despite frequent references to it by many not-so-well informed authors.

Lower deck in frigates

As frigates did not carry guns on their lower decks they were planked entirely in deal, apart from the waterways and binding strakes which were of oak. The *shutting in* was also of deal of the same thickness as the flat, with the exception of the midships strake which was sometimes 1in thicker to pillar on.

Middle deck in three-deckers

The usual practice was for the middle deck in three-deckers to have the waterways, binding strakes, outermost strakes and the forward part of the flat as far aft as the after end of the galley, made of oak, with the rest of the deck of deal. The shutting in was also of deal, of the same thickness as the flat, with the midships strake or strakes 1in thicker to support the pillars.

vessels, the proportions of the waterways varied in the different types.

From the thickest part, which coincided with the inboard face of the *spirketting*, '(Traditional Wooden Shipbuilding' Part 6 MS 57), it was chined down to the thickness of the flat. The outer part, where it came beneath the spirketting, was bearded back between ³⁄₈in and ³⁄₄in. This was done for two reasons. First, the upwards slope made it easier to caulk the seam and second, in the event of defective caulking, any water which penetrated the seam would tend to drain down between the frames, to the limbers.

Just outboard of the main hatchway coaming were two *binding strakes* running the whole length of the deck. These could either be the two strakes immediately adjacent to the hatchway coaming, or the second and third strakes from it. They were of oak, 1in thicker than the rest of the flat and

were let down between the beams in order to maintain a flush deck.

Between the binding strakes and the waterway the deck was mainly planked with deal, with the exception of the outermost strakes, which being subject to greater wear and tear from the guns, were generally of oak. Usually four in number, but five in three-deckers and three in sloops, they were often worked top and butt for extra strength.

As always there were many exceptions. Some ships, particularly the smaller ones, had their upper decks planked entirely with deals. On many the *first shift* of planking was of oak, as well as the outermost strakes, with the remainder of deal (fig 2). (*First shift* means the first lengths of planks from forward.)

Inboard of the binding strakes the deck was *shut in* between the various hatchways, ladderways, mast partners, etc, by means of short deals of the same thickness as the flat.

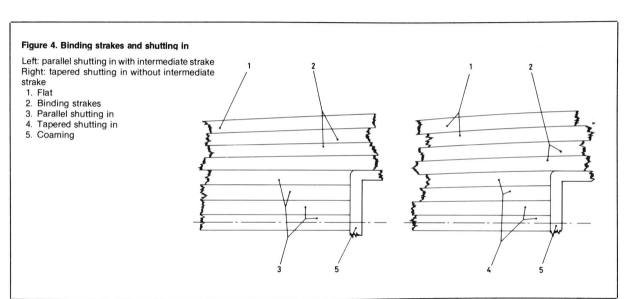

Figure 4. Binding strakes and shutting in

Left: parallel shutting in with intermediate strake
Right: tapered shutting in without intermediate strake
1. Flat
2. Binding strakes
3. Parallel shutting in
4. Tapered shutting in
5. Coaming

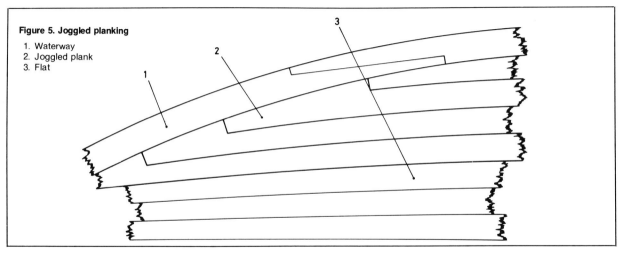

Figure 5. Joggled planking

1. Waterway
2. Joggled plank
3. Flat

Orlops and platforms

In two- and three-decked ships the orlop was a continuous deck with a slight round up, usually of 2in throughout its length. In frigates the orlop ran from abaft the fore hatchway to the fore side of the after hatchway. It too had a round up of 2in. Ahead of the fore hatchway and abaft the after hatchway frigates had platforms, called the fore and after platforms respectively. These had no round up and were planked throughout with 1½in deals, with no waterways or binding strakes. The fore and after parts of the orlops of two- and three-deckers were planked in the same way but with 2in deals.

The orlops in the early frigates were not planked at all. They were used solely for the stowage of the ship's anchor cables and were left unplanked to facilitate drainage to the bilges below. By the 1760s frigates had adopted the system of orlop planking that was used between the fore and after hatchways in the orlops of larger ships. Outboard of the side tier carlings the planking followed the same pattern as the platforms, or the ends of the full length orlops.

Between these carlings a different system was used. Here the coamings and side tier carlings, together with the beams, were rabetted, with the intermediate carlings being let down the same amount. The rabetts were usually ½ to 1in deeper than the thickness of the planking, short lengths of which were laid between the beams (fig 3). This planking was of the same thickness as that of the corresponding orlop or platforms. It was laid in this way so that it could be easily lifted to gain access to the large water and beer casks in the hold below.

Quarterdeck, forecastle and roundhouse

The planking of the forecastle was similar to that of the quarterdeck. In both cases, in all ships of 24 guns and above, there was a 4in waterway chined down to a 3in flat. One or two strakes next to the waterway were of oak but the rest of the flat was deal. There were no binding strakes.

The planking of the roundhouse followed the same pattern but in this case the flat was 2½in thick and was entirely of deal. Waterways remained at 4in and were of oak.

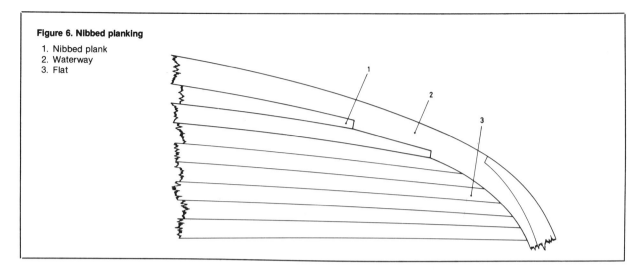

Figure 6. Nibbed planking

1. Nibbed plank
2. Waterway
3. Flat

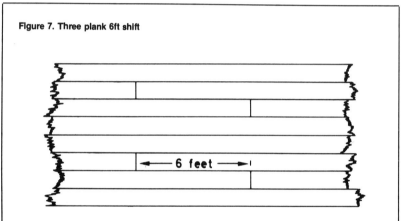

Figure 7. Three plank 6ft shift

← 6 feet →

Laying the deck

The tapering of planks towards the ends of the ship has already been mentioned. There were a few exceptions to this, however, the major one being the waterways. These remained the same width for their whole length. Binding strakes were usually tapered but they could be parallel throughout. In some ships the planks of the *shutting in* were not tapered, which meant that the inboard face of the binding strakes was parallel to the middle line, even though the binding strakes themselves might be tapered. In others the *shutting* in planks were also tapered, with the result that the inner face of the binding strakes curved in towards the middle line at the extremities (fig 4).

When the shape of the deck aft was such that the planks required excessive tapering and/or curvature the planks were *joggled* where they met the water-way (fig 5). The forward part of the deck presented a different problem as here the breadth of the deck tapered to a blunt point. To work the planks into this would have meant that they would have needed abnormal curvature and would have ended in sharp points. The answer was to give the planks a moderate curvature and to snape their ends and fay them to the waterway. Where the length of the snape exceeded four times its width, the end was cut square and snaped to half its width. It was then *nibbed* or let into the waterway (fig 6).

Shift of butts

The most difficult part of laying a deck was to work out the shift of butts, in other words to establish where the plank ends should butt one against the other. First of all the butts had to lie on a beam, in order that they could be adequately supported and secured.

Ideally they should be worked to a *three plank shift*, which meant that there should be three whole planks between any two butts on the same beam. Second, the butts had to *overlaunch* or be *shifted* at least 6ft. That is to say that the butts in any two adjacent planks should not be closer together than 6ft (fig 7).

The next requirement was that the butts should not be adjacent to openings in the deck such as hatchways, mast partners etc, or come under standards. One of the butts of the waterways had to coincide with the pump scupper, in order that the timber should not be unduly weakened by cutting the scupper through it. In addition all the butts of the waterways had to 'give good shift' to the butts of the spirketting.

A further complication arose because the beams were not spaced equally, this being particularly so in the way of the main hatchway and mainmast, where there were beam arms instead of complete beams. In this area it was virtually impossible to get a good shift with short English oak plank and so the binding strakes were usually made from the longer Dantzic oak. Inboard of the binding strakes there were no problems, as the shutting in only required short lengths and there were therefore no butts.

Outboard of the binding strakes, where the flat was frequently of deal, the problem was simpler as there was a greater choice of plank lengths. Even so it was sometimes necessary to use an occasional two- plank shift in order to get a good shift with the outboard strakes. This was particularly so where the latter were worked top and butt with English oak and had themselves to give good shift to the waterways. Figs 8 and 9 show the after and forward parts of the lower deck of a 38-gun frigate and illustrate the final result.

The next article in the series, in *Model Shipwright* 65 will continue this description of the structure of the decks and will deal with such things as hatchway coamings, mast partners etc.

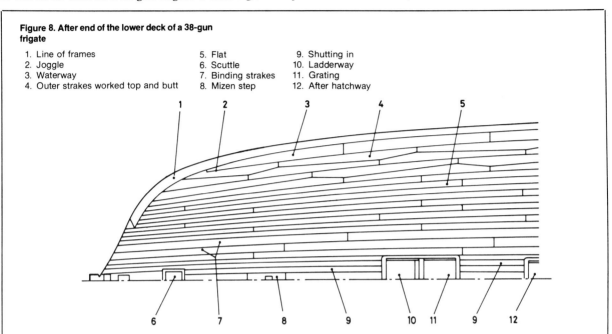

Figure 8. After end of the lower deck of a 38-gun frigate

1. Line of frames
2. Joggle
3. Waterway
4. Outer strakes worked top and butt
5. Flat
6. Scuttle
7. Binding strakes
8. Mizen step
9. Shutting in
10. Ladderway
11. Grating
12. After hatchway

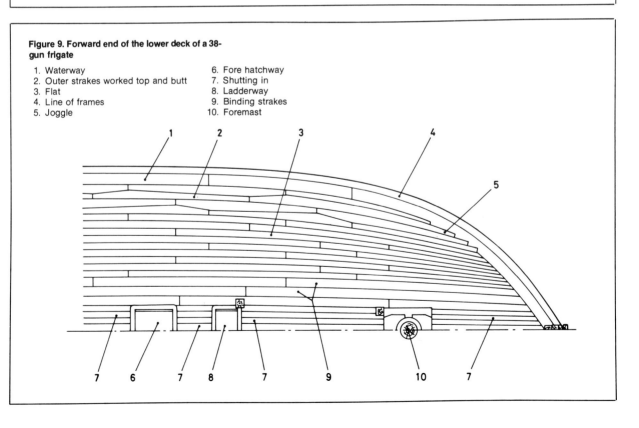

Figure 9. Forward end of the lower deck of a 38-gun frigate

1. Waterway
2. Outer strakes worked top and butt
3. Flat
4. Line of frames
5. Joggle
6. Fore hatchway
7. Shutting in
8. Ladderway
9. Binding strakes
10. Foremast

MINIATURE MERCHANTMEN

Carmania

CUNARD LINER (1905)

by John Bowen

When they entered Cunard's transatlantic service in 1905 they were often referred to as 'the pretty sisters'. These were, of course, the *Caronia* and *Carmania*, built by John Brown & Co at Clydebank.

In the early years of this century the Cunard Company, faced with intense competition on the North Atlantic from lines with larger and more modern vessels, was actively engaged in seeking ways and means to remedy this situation. In the longer term their aim was to build two large express pas-senger ships, but in the meantime they had ordered from John Brown a pair of intermediate liners, an answer no doubt to the White Star Line's *Cedric* and *Celtic*. One of the many very urgent matters exercising the Company's mind was the type of propelling machinery to be installed in the proposed express ships. The two intermediates, *Caronia* and *Carmania*, were to be driven by twin screw quadruple expansion machinery.

The steam turbine was proving its worth in cross-channel vessels. Could it, Cunard wondered, be adapted for use in large, fast ocean-going passenger liners? They set up a committee to investigate the possibility, and John Brown & Co put forward the suggestion that turbine machinery be installed in the *Carmania*. This would give practi-

Carmania as completed. In this photo the three forward boats are shown in the outboard position, as mentioned in the text. Though not easily seen they are secured by diagonal crossed gripes.

cal experience of large turbines, and also provide comparison with a similar ship propelled by conventional means. In due course, Cunard decided to accept this proposal, and *Carmania* was completed as a triple screw ship with compound turbines. On subsequent trials and in service she was found to have the edge over her sister ship.

Externally, above water (below water the hull at the after end had to be modified to accommodate the third, centre line, propeller) there was little difference between the two ships. One noticeable feature was that on *Caronia's* Shelter Deck forward many of the larger ventilators were fitted with Gibbs extractor type heads, whereas on *Carmania* these had cowl tops. *Caronia* was completed with the black topside paint carried up to the level of the Bridge Deck, but on *Carmania* it stopped one deck down at Shelter Deck level. Subsequently, *Caronia's* black topside paint was lowered to this deck level. However, later photographs of the two ships show from time to time some variation in the line of division between hull black and superstructure white.

Caronia (Yard No 362) was completed in February 1905 and *Carmania* (Yard No 366) in November 1905. Both ships were placed on Cunard's Liverpool-New York service. Upon the outbreak of hostilities in August 1914 they were taken up by the Government and rapidly fitted out as armed merchant cruisers, *Carmania* being given eight old 4.7in guns. A month later she was in the South Atlantic and on 14 September surprised the German auxiliary cruiser *Cap Trafalgar* (completed early in 1914 for the Hamburg-South America Line) at Trinidade Island off the coast of Brazil. She had been hastily fitted out some days earlier with two 4.1in guns and a number of 3.7mm pom-pom type heavy machine guns. The engagement which followed has been well documented. Suffice to say that both vessels were heavily damaged and suffered casualties, and it ended with the *Cap Trafalgar* sinking. *Carmania* went to Gibraltar for repairs, where the 4.7in guns were replaced with 6in guns, and she resumed her patrols. In 1916 the sisters were returned to Cunard, and spent the remaining war years mainly on trooping duties.

Immediately after the Armistice, *Carmania* was given a quick refit and returned to the Liverpool-New York run. In 1923, she was sent back to her builders for a thorough overhaul and conversion to a cabin class ship. During this refit the life-saving gear was renewed and increased, luffing davits replacing the original radial davits, and double banked boats were stowed under all davits except at the forward and after positions where there was a single boat over a collapsible boat.

Both ships continued to be employed mainly on the Company's UK-USA/Canada services until 1931 when they were withdrawn and laid up. *Carmania* was sold the following year to Hughes Bolckow & Co and broken up at Blyth, Northumberland. *Caronia* was also sold to the same company, but was resold by them to Japanese breakers; she was broken up at Osaka in 1933.

Basic data

Length overall 672ft 6in
Length between perpendiculars 650ft 0in
Breadth moulded 72ft 0in
Draught 33ft 3in
Tonnage 19,524 tons gross
Cargo capacity approx 10,000 tons
Displacement at load draught 30,918 tons
Machinery 1 HP and 2 LP turbines = 18,900 shp
Speed 18 knots

A few other details may be of passing interest. Some 12,000 tons of steel and 1,800,000 rivets were used in her construction. The shell plating ranged from 13/20in to $1\frac{1}{8}$ in thickness, and the largest plates could weigh over $3\frac{1}{2}$ tons. In building the turbines 1,150,000 blades were individually fitted and checked. Notwithstanding the large carrying capacity, the hull had fairly fine lines and a correspondingly low (for this type of ship) coefficient of fineness ('block coefficient') of just below 0.7.

The model

The plan is reproduced full size of a 1/1200 scale waterline model of the ship as completed. It can also be used for a model of *Caronia*, but in this case the eight cowl ventilators on the Shelter Deck forward – see sectional profile – should be given Gibbs type heads, and the black topside paint carried one deck higher if it is to be of the ship as built.

There are two ways of carving the hull: either to the level of the Shelter Deck, or to the level of the Bridge Deck, in which case the block will have to be cut down forward and aft to the line of the Shelter Deck. The bow has an easy flare, as can be seen from the sections. Great care must be taken when carving the counter stern to maintain its exact profile and plan. This is a feature of the ship, especially when viewed from certain angles, and failure to reproduce it correctly, especially in profile, can mar the appearance of the model very considerably. If the first method is adopted for carving the hull, the long midship deckhouse is added separately. Once it has been fitted, the edge each side can be faced with a strip of mounted wood shaving extended upwards to form the bulwark running the length of the Bridge Deck, and also extended at each end to form the short bulwarks on the Shelter Deck. The forward and after ends of the strip, once they have been shaped (before it is fixed in place) can be faced in the same way. The width and length of this strip must be such as to allow for the thickness of the mounted shaving being used. The line of the butt of the shaving with the edge of the hull, once the shaving has been sanded flush and smooth with the hull, provides a good painting guide line between black and white. If portholes are pierced through the shaving before it is fitted, then the edges of the wood strip should be painted dark grey.

The upperworks present few problems, being mainly a series of rectangular units. The two thin 'tails' at the after end of the forward house on the Boat Deck are best added as separate pieces, as are the two bay window extensions on the next house aft. The same goes for the light-and-air trunks on each side of the funnel casings and that of the engine room skylight, since they are only 4ft high by 2ft wide, and have a sloping top.

Fittings

As well as the ten Gibbs extractor ventilators (two forward and eight aft) there are a number of cowl ventilators to be made, the most prominent of which are the large ones fitted on top of the eight rectangular ventilators to the stokeholds. Their cowls are 6ft 6in diameter, and the trunks 4ft 6in diameter. The hollowed out half seed on a piece of dowel stem is one way of making these. Being a very prominent feature of the ship care must be taken

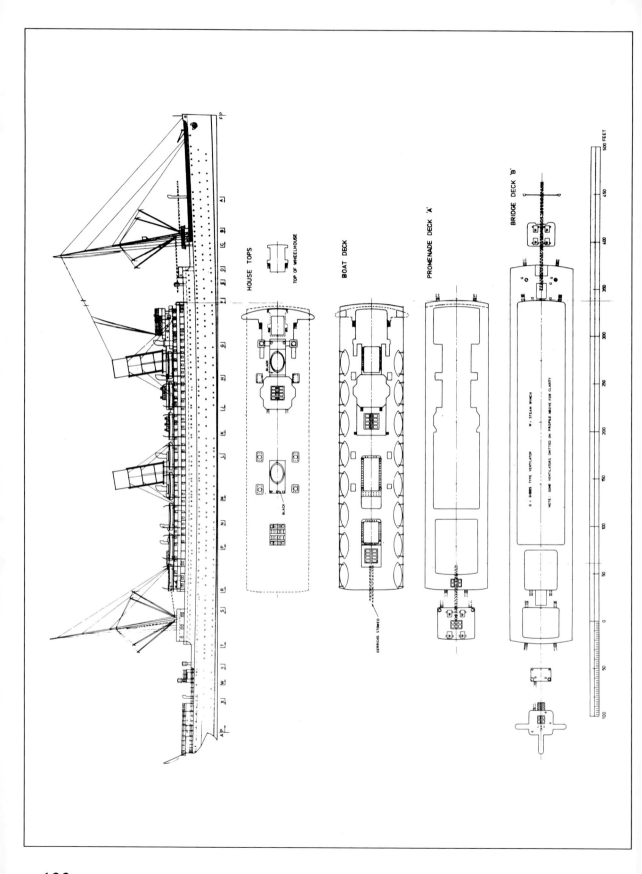

HOUSE TOPS

TOP OF WHEELHOUSE

BOAT DECK

PROMENADE DECK 'A'

BRIDGE DECK 'B'

DERRICKS STOWED

G = GIBBS TYPE VENTILATOR   W = STEAM WINCH

NOTE: SOME VENTILATORS OMITTED ON PROFILE ABOVE FOR CLARITY

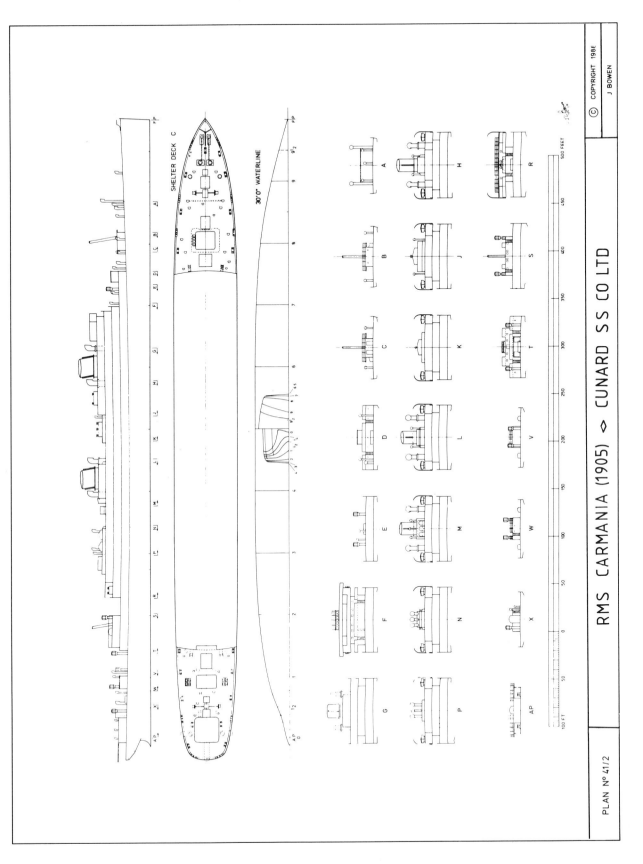

SHELTER DECK C

30'0" WATERLINE

RMS CARMANIA (1905) ◇ CUNARD SS CO LTD

PLAN Nº 41/2

to obtain complete uniformity in shape and height. (Note: because of their numbers only a few of the ventilators have been included on the outboard profile, but they are shown on the sectional profile, which should be used to obtain their heights). Several of the skylights have small mushroom top ventilators placed along their centre line.

The anchors are handled by cable lifters instead of a windlass, and there are three steam warping winches, two forward and one aft, and ten steam winches for handling cargo.

The funnels can be made by squeezing a piece of brass tube of the right diameter, if such is available, to produce their elliptical cross section. It would have to be about 0.16in (4mm) external diameter. The alternative is to carve a length of wood to the elliptical shape, wax it and wind three or four turns of thin paper round it, gluing as it is wound on, and finishing with the cut end on the after side of the funnel, where it will be hidden by a waste steam pipe. If one end of this piece of stick is cut square, and the other end cut to the rake of the funnel, this will facilitate trimming the ends of the paper tube correctly. An allowance will have to be made when shaping this stick to allow for the thicknesses of paper being used. The three black bands can be of wire, painted black, and put on after the funnels have been painted. Note that the distance between the bands is the same, but that the distance from the top of the funnel down to the first band is slightly greater. The funnels sit on elliptical bases 5ft high, the sides of which are

The ship again as built. A Gibbs type ventilator can be seen on the Bridge (B) Deck (below the wheelhouse).

Photographs from the author's collection

vertical, and with a prominent rim or top piece 12in deep. The funnels and masts have the same rake.

The sixteen lifeboats are carried under ordinary radial davits. Both the rigging plan, general arrangement plan and some photographs show the forward three boats on each side swung outboard and secured by two crossed gripes. Other photographs show these same boats stowed inboard on deck in the usual way. From the modelling point of view the latter is an easier arrangement.

Painting

Hull black above waterline to level of Shelter Deck, red below waterline; narrow white ribband between black and red
Superstructure white
Wheelhouse mahogany
Deckhouses white
Inside bulwarks white
Boats, davits white, boats have mahogany sheerstrake, plain canvas covers without tabs.
Ventilators white, red inside cowls
Masts, derricks, vent derrick posts golden brown
Hatches golden brown
Cable lifters, winches, capstans, bollards, fairleads black
Funnels Cunard red, black top, three narrow black bands
Skylights dark brown

Water tanks white
Anchor crane white
Decks all planked

References

Plans: Some shipbuilder's plans have survived and are held by the Glasgow University Archives (write to The Archivist, The Archives, The University, Glasgow G12 8QQ, Scotland, for a list). The list of plans does not show a rigging plan for either vessel, and on the profile drawings the funnels and masts are 'chopped off' short just above deck level. In case anyone is wondering about the heights of the masts and funnels on my drawing, these are based on data given in a contemporary technical journal, and later cross-checked when a copy of the shipbuilder's rigging plan for *Carmania* came my way.

Descriptive articles: The journal *Engineering* contains the following:
10 Feb 1905 page 188 et seq *The New Cunard Liners*; includes a full page broadside picture of *Caronia* on trials.
24 Feb 1905 pp 260-1 *Passenger accommodation on Caronia*.
3 March 1905 p 291. Launch of the *Carmania*, with starboard quarter photo of the vessel on the stocks.
1 December 1905 pp 715-725 article and photos of *Carmania*.
Note: none of the above articles contain general arrangement plans or profile drawings of either ship.

Photographs: The Scottish Record Office (address: Scottish Record Office, HM General Register Office, Edinburgh EH1 3YY, Scotland) holds a number of photographs of the two ships, but as *Caronia* was completed first the majority are of this ship. The most useful are:
No 123/8 bow view of *Carmania* leaving fitting out basin.
The following are all for *Caronia*
86/10, 86/12-14 on board deck views.
115/6 three-quarter starboard bow view of ship on trials.
185/13 nearly full port broadside view of ship on trials (taken from forward of midships).
205/7 port side of ship from after funnel to stern, taken from across the fitting out basin.
304/13 looking aft along the Boat Deck, port side.
304/14 close up at front of bridge superstructure from Shelter Deck.

General: General information and basic data about the two ships can be found in such works as:
Sea Breezes Volume 29 (March issue) 1960, p 208. Article on the *Carmania* by J H Isherwood in his *Steamers of the Past* series.
The Cunard Story by Howard Johnson (Whittet Books Ltd, London. 1987).
North Atlantic Seaway by N R P Bonsor
Great Passenger Ships of the World Volume I by A Kludas
An account of her action with the *Cap Trafalgar* is contained in *Armed Merchant Cruisers* by Kenneth Poolman (Leo Cooper/Secker & Warburg, 1985). In passing it should be mentioned that he gives the date of her disposal incorrectly as 1925.

XEBEC
Mistique
of 1762

by Peter Heriz-Smith

Model of a French tartane by the author, showing sail 'stitching' and unrealistic positioning of lateen sails.

The notes which follow are inspired by my latest model – a French-built xebec, built to a scale of 1/192. To those who have taken an interest in these Mediterranean craft, the model may appear a bit strange; and so, in many ways, it is, for it does not conform to the popular conception of what the xebec looked like.

First, though, let us turn to a contemporary definition in William Falconer's *Marine Dictionary* of 1769. The xebec, he writes, is,

...a small three-masted vessel, navigated in the Mediterranean Sea, also on the coasts of Spain, Portugal, and Barbary, and was distinguished from all other European vessels by the great projection of the prow and stern beyond the cutwater and stern-post respectively ... Being generally equipped as a corsair, it was constructed with a very narrow floor, to be more swift in pursuit of the enemy; and of a great breadth to enable her to carry a considerable force of sail for this purpose, without danger of overturning. As these vessels were usually very low built, their decks were formed with a very great convexity from the middle of their breadth towards the sides, in order to carry off the water, which fell aboard, more readily by their scuppers. But as this convexity rendered it very difficult to walk thereon at sea,

particularly when the vessel rolled heavily, there was a platform of grating extending along the deck from the sides of the vessel towards the middle, and the water could pass through the grating to the scuppers ... [*this was also essential as a gun platform. Without it, the guns could not have been elevated above horiztonal. EPH-S*] ... When a xebec was equipped for war, she sometimes navigated by three different methods, according to the force or direction of the wind. Thus, when the wind was fair, and nearly astern, it was usual to extend square sails upon the mainmast; and, indeed, frequently upon the foremast: and as those sails were rarely used in a scant wind, they were of extraordinary breadth. When the wind was unfavourable to the course, and yet continued moderate, the square yards and sails were removed from the mast, and laid by, in order to make way for the large lateen sails and yards, which soon assumed their place; but if the foul wind increased to a storm, these latter were also lowered and displaced; and small lateen yards and proportional sails were extended on all masts.

The xebecs, which were generally armed as vessels of war by the Algerians, mounted from sixteen to twenty-four cannon, and carried from 300 to 450 men, two thirds of whom were generally soldiers.

The method of working these vessels was so exceedingly complicated and difficult, that the labour was very considerable.

The xebec, then, was basically a North African type of vessel which was ideally suited to its role as an armed raider agianst against the French coast and coastal shipping. It was light and fast, and its shallow draught enabled it to escape into waters inaccessible to the normal warship, and, being equipped with oars, it was not vulnerable in a dead calm.

In Plate LVIII of his *Architectura Navalis Mercatoria* of 1768, Fredrik Henrik af Chapman shows a detail plan of one of these Algerian xebecs which brings out clearly the traditional details of hull construction described by Falconer. This plan was reproduced and used by R J Collins for his model in the Science Museum.

The xebec was, in short, a serious hit-and-run threat, and in 1750 Antoine-Louis de Rouillé, in order to try to fight fire with fire, commissioned four of these vessels for the *Marine Royale*. The French shipwrights of Toulon, however, had no experience of building them, so he called on the services of the acknowleged experts from Majorca under one Joseph Caubet. (It is interesting to note that even experts are fallible. It is recorded by R de Lagarlière that the Majorcans made the launching ways too shallow, with the result that the completed hulls could not at first be launched. There is no record of the reaction of the local Toulonnais shipwrights, but one can imagine that it was more ribald than sympathetic.)

Two of these xebecs, *Requin* (Shark) and *Indescret*, were of 260 tons each and armed with twenty-four guns. The other two, *Rusé* (The Cunning One) and *Serpent*, were quite a bit smaller, of 150 tons and eighteen guns.

In the Musée de la Marine in Paris, there is a very fine large contemporary model which undoubtedly represents one of the two larger craft. Although I was at the time researching material for my galley. *La Réale*, I was fascinated by the sheer beauty of the xebec model. After buying the very good plans issued by the Association des Amis des Musées de la Marine, I spent a long time examining it with sketch-book in hand. As a result, I was able later to build a plank-on-frame model of my own.

This was long before the publication in 1987 of the monograph by Hubert Berti on the *Requin*, accompanied by Jean Boudriot's superb set of plans. I was relieved to find that this publication did not invalidate my own model, but it is now essential reading for any future builder.

The 'glass-case' method of presenting the rig shows the lateen yards and sails slung fore and aft amidships, and inside the tackles supporting the masts. This is visually satisfying, but in view of the complications of actually sailing the vessel, it is rather like displaying a bird with folded-wings; but I cannot think of any other way of doing it in a static model.

It is clear from the Falconer description and from contemporary engravings that:

- A xebec under way carried its lateen sails forward of the masts and outside the supporting rigging.

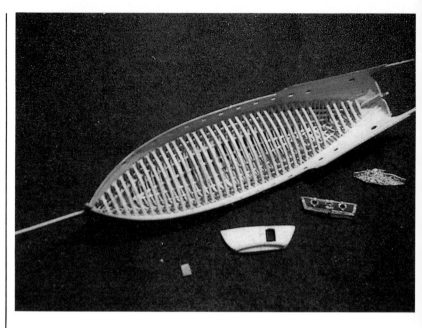

- To go about, the yard had to be drawn by tackles to the vertical and man-oeuvred round to the opposite side of the mast, an operation which would be impossible if the masts were supported by permanent shrouds; hence the tackles, fastened to toggles for quick release (Figure 1).
- This system of tackles and toggles

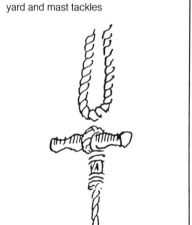

Figure 1 Toggle for quick-release of yard and mast tackles

did not afford very strong support to the masts, which therefore had to be on the massive side. Their weight and the pressure of the huge lateen sails made it essential to reinforce the deck of the shallow hull, especially in the way of the foremast

A model by the author of a xebec of 1750 in frame, and showing the light construction.

stepped in the eyes of the vessel.
- Because of the number of inter-changeable yards and sails, they all had to be capable of rapid and easy exchange, and so, the yards, too, were attached to the lifts by toggles.
- Since there was no system of ratlines, reefing and furling of lateen sails was effected by members of the crew – probably boys – shinning up the yard itself. This is the practise on dhows to this day.
- The stowage of the spare yards and sails must have caused problems, and considerable clutter on deck.

Few of these complications can be shown on a model in such a way as to explain them to viewers lacking specialist knowledge.

The French xebec

So far I have dealt with what I would call the traditional xebec rig described by Falconer, but there were many variations. Some xebecs were lateen rigged on the foremast and square rigged on the main, or vice versa. Others, keeping the traditional hull configuration, were square-rigged throughout. This brings us back to the subject in hand.

The four Majorcan-built xebecs

The author's model of a xebec of 1750.

proved to be successful, so in 1762 four more were commissioned. This time, however, the Toulon shipwrights saw no reason why they should not do the job themselves. Another Musée model portrays one of these, *le Singe*, and a drawing expressly based on this model is produced by Admiral Paris – he calls it the *Mistique*, though none of the four new vessels bore this name.

His plan shows a much sturdier and more European method of hull construction. Instead of the Majorcan light frames there are heavy double frames, and the deck completely lacks the extreme rise of beam which is characteristic of the traditional craft. Apart from this, the hull and deck reinforcements are clearly in the xebec pattern.

The sail plan is, however, completely different. The foremast carries the traditional lateen rig with normal lateen tackles, toggle connection, etc. There is a large foresail extended to the bowsprit. The mainmast, however, is a polacca– a polemast. This is supported to lower yard level by a stay and shrouds with normal deadeye connections. Above this, in way of the tops

and topgallant, the mast is unsupported. The advantages of this polacca mast are comparative lightness, and the ease with which the yards can be sent down. On the other hand, it is vulnerable in foul weather, and repairs to it at sea are almost impossible. The plan shows the shrouds rattled down; the museum model does not, a difference which is insignificant, since ships alter during their lifetime. In the model, access aloft is by ladder aft of the mast.

The mizzen is different again. It consists of a lower and upper mast doubled between cap and spreaders, with shrouds to both. The upper mast carries a square sail, and the lower a full lateen yard carrying only a loose-footed spanker aft. The overall appearance of these three disparate rigs in a single hull is almost uncomfortably peculiar. It is fairly certain that this mongrel rig was not successful. At least, no more xebecs were commissioned for the French navy after 1779 when these last four were taken out of service. Xebecs did not disappear from the Mediterranean, of course, and Admiral Paris shows detailed plans of a

late example called *Boberach*, captured from the Algerians in 1830.

Anyway, I decided that a model of the *Singe/Mistique* would be interesting if built as a waterline version to a scale of 1/192. I included detail missing from the plan and, indeed, from the Musée model, such as cannon and swivel guns, ship's boat and anchors.

A number of crew were included, but I made no attempt to represent a full complement, which on the prototype numbered over 200 officers, sailors, boys and soldiers. So far I have not added any spare sails and spars but I feel that I shall have to put a couple on board somewhere.

The model

There is little to comment upon in the building of the model, and on the whole I used the techniques outlined in my notes on the sixteenth century English ship in *MS 65*, but I included a couple of refinements which I think are an improvement.

It will be recalled that I moulded the

The completed model of *Mistique*, **with its interesting mixed rig.**

sails over waxed formers and set them with acrylic medium. I indicated the cloths with slight pencil lines. Instead of these, I now substituted printed stitching by a method I had already successfully used in a model of a tartane. I set a 20mm circular saw blade from my miniature electric drill on its mandrell into a length of aluminium tube. This I rolled over an ordinary rubber-stamp pad, and transferred the impression along the lines of the cloths. The resulting effect of miniscule stitching is excellent, and I can recommend the method to others working to a small scale. Care is needed, of course, especially when matching the stitching to the obverse side of a sail, and the saw serrations need to be kept clean.

Once again I wanted to set the model in a transparent 'sea' in order not to lose the underwater hull so, as before, I cut out the waterline shape of the hull

from a sheet of acrylic plastic. Previously, I flowed cellulose dope over this to prevent too glassy a surface. For the xebec I found some clear plastic left over from a temporary double-glazing job, and I crumpled, twisted and generally tortured it until it was a mass of tiny facets. This I glued to the edges only of the acrylic sheet, and in doing so gained some useful hints of a swell. The hull cavity was cut about ⅛in smaller all round than the one below it, and this ensured an undetectable join between hull and 'water', besides indicating some useful disturbance of the water around the hull. A few touches of solid white acrylic paint completed the job. The effect of moving and sparkling water was better than I had hoped, and at this scale seemed more convincing than a carved and painted sea.

Rigging was mostly of thread, but painted wire was used in areas where curves were important. A prominent example is the forestay. It carried a foresail, and the combined pressure of this and of the enormous lateen on the

mast was bound to slacken the tautness of the stay. Only wire could be relied on to portray this important feature.

I find the lateen rig endlessly fascinating. It may have its limitations and drawbacks, but the raking sweep of the yards and sails afford a most satisfying counterpoint to the sheer of the hull below, and the very names of the lateeners are as excitingly exotic as the vessels are beautiful. From Arabia one can work through the alphabet from the *balam*, the *boom* and *bedam* to the *sambuk*, *zara* and *zaruk*. Feluccas, garassas and *nuggers* sailed the Nile. From India came the *dhoni*, the *batella*, the *pattaman*. The Turks built the *mahouna*, the Portuguese the *caravel* (though the *Nina* had to abandon the lateen for Atlantic voyaging). Throughout the Mediterranean there were galleys, galiotes, pinques, tartanes and, of course xebecs. It is a long list, and I have not mentioned them all.

The rig spread across the Atlantic to the Great Lakes, the north to Danish, Russian and Finnish waters. European ships carried it on the mizzen, and to this day lateener dhows ply between Lamu, Mombasa and the Red Sea. The rig is still employed on the hard-chine fishing dhows on Lake Victoria, and even appears in a rather ragged form on the mangrove pole masts of outriggers on the East African coast.

Historically, during the Crusades, the Venetians supplied (at a price) galleys and lumbering lateen rigged cavalry transports to the Christian armies, and an interesting study of early amphibious warfare in the thirteenth and fourteenth centuries could be made, when Greek Fire, mangonels and petraries were the artillery, and the lateen spars were adapted to assault on harbour fortifications ... but I am guilty of rambling into the byways of nautical research – which is part of the pleasure!

Sources

Chébecs et Bâtiments Méditerranéans Le Requin 1750 by Jean Boudriot and Hubert Berti (Collection Archéologie Navale 1987). This must be the ultimate standard work. It is full of information, pictures and photographs, plus a set of Boudriot's customary fully-detailed plans.
Chebec de 24 Canons XVIII Siècle (Association des Amis des Musées de la Marine, Paris). After the Boudriot drawings mentioned above this is the best plan available, and is accompanied by a useful monograph by R de Lagarlière, and photographs of the museum model.

This overhead view shows the effectiveness of the author's method of representing the sea.

Architectura Navalis Mercatoria by Hendrik af Chapman (Robert Loef Verlag, Magdeburg) contains a plan of an Algerian xebec.
Souvenirs de Marine by Admiral Paris (Editions des 4 Seigneurs, Grenoble 1975). Plan of the *Mistique*, copies of the Algerian xebec from Chapman, and an interesting plan of a later Algerian xebec c1830.
The Ship by Björn Langstrom (Allen & Unwin). Useful for the reconstruction of lateeners of various epochs.

The Dhow by Clifford W Hawkins (Nautical Publishing Co Ltd, 1977). A beautifully illustrated survey of these craft.
Chronicles of the Crusades by Joinville & Villehardouin (Penguin Classics). Has interesting reports of amphibious warfare against the Turks and Saracens.

Some details of the deck layout of the vessel.

Photographs are by the author and John Bowen

STERN WHEELER
Far West

by William Wiseman

So-called 'mountain boats' were vessels of a unique design for travelling on the small, shallow, snag-infested rivers and tributaries of the western territories of the United States, having evolved from the earlier western river steamboats of the Ohio and Mississippi Rivers. They were smaller, slower, lighter and far less glamorous than the floating palaces of the Mississippi. All were sternwheelers, shallow water design with a draught so small that many tons of cargo could be carried on only a few feet of water. Their bows were shaped like a spoon for sliding over shoals and the oversized paddlewheel that dipped only a few inches into the water was powered by two high-pressure steam engines. They could travel onto the most difficult small rivers and feeders where no other powered vessel could go.

Far West was a typical boat of this class. Her length was 190ft, beam 33ft and she drew only 20in of water empty or could carry 398 tons of cargo with a draught of 4ft 6in. Her hull was framed in oak with the sides and bottom planked in pine or poplar for lightness. She carried four rudders, hung side by side from the transom directly ahead of the paddlewheel mounted on a full stern. The two inboard rudders were of the balanced type (the lower portion extending forward of the tiller post) connected to tiller arms, while the two outboard rudders were unbalanced. All four rudders were connected in parallel with wooden connecting arms, to serve as one single massive rudder. Her paddlewheel was 18ft in diameter, 24ft wide and

The port bow, showing foredeck details.

A general view of the fore end showing details of rigging, deck cargo and stacked wood for firing the boiler. Note the figure seated in the chair.

belted with cast iron. Two engines, 15in bore × 5ft stroke, drove the wheel at 20rpm, which would make a paddle dip into the water 260 times per minute, and provide enough thrust to overcome currents in excess of 10mph. Her three boilers (with two flues each) measured 33ft × 22ft, and produced a working pressure of 130psi.

Her cost was $24,000. Such a low figure makes one wonder at the rather loose manner in which these vessels were built and operated, giving rise to a high rate of boat and cargo loss. However, one full cargo trip often paid entirely for the boat, and any extra was profit for the company; economically speaking, such a policy made practical business sense.

Far West was built in Pittsburgh,

Close up details of the deck cargo and boiler fuel.

The middle section of the model, showing more cargo, the deckhouse and the wheelhouse with the large diameter wheel just visible.

The ship's boat. The open door leads to the engine room.

Pennsylvania, in 1870, for the Coulson Packet Company and designed to operate on the upper Missouri and Yellowstone Rivers in the northwestern territories.

During this period, the US Government leased (or commandeered) steamboats for the supply and transportation of troops necessary to overcome the Indian opposition to western expansion. Since each steamboat owner was paid from $300 to $350 per day per boat, they were quite happy to oblige with

the use of their boats.

Due to hostile Indians, western land surveys had to be accomplished by the US Army, at times running roughshod over the Indians' land. In 1872 General David S Stanley, along with Lieutenant Colonel George A Custer, commanded the first survey's escort to the Yellowstone Valley, located in the Montana Territory. This expedition was accomplished with the help of three mountain steamboats: *Far West, Key West*, and *Peninah*. It is believed that Custer was carried by *Far West*.

She was then released from the government service and retained under the command of Captain Marsh, one of the two greatest steamboat men of the West; the other was Captain Joseph Marie La Barge.

Four years later she was commandeered again to transport Custer and units of the 7th Cavalry to quell once more the hostile Sioux Indians; the result was the disastrous defeat for Custer at Little Big Horn. *Far West* entered the history

The port stern quarter with details of the paddle wheel, various trusses and bracing wires. Two of the four rudders are visible. Note the engineer examining part of the machinery through the opening in the side of the house.

books by setting the record for the fastest and wildest steamboat trip on the Missouri River, carrying the battle wounded and the news of the defeat to Fort Lincoln.

During repairs, she had an extra deck added (hurricane roof) for the convenience of the passengers, which markedly changed her appearance.

Later in 1876, she carried General Miles and Buffalo Bill on a scouting trip, as well as transporting the Indian Peace Commission on a mission to establish another peace treaty with the Indians.

The last mass leasing of steamboats by the government was for the purpose of carrying the Sioux and Cheyenne Indians to the Standing Rock Reservation, in which *Far West*

was one of the three boats used.

Later she was sold to Victor Bonnet and Captain Dodds and on October 20 1883, while downward bound for St Louis, *Far West* struck a snag and sank; a total loss.

The model

The model was constructed to ¹/₈ in = 1ft (1/96 scale) using plans drawn by John L. Fryant. The hull is a wood frame with basswood sub planking to which all exterior planking is fastened.

I chose to model *Far West* using various hardwoods sealed with Danish Watco Natural Oil to preserve the beauty of the wood and to create a pleasing appearance, rather than having the usual stark white colour scheme of contemporary steamboat models.

Mild steel was used for most of the metal parts, finished by heating until the proper colour was obtained or by simply letting the metal weather itself for a period of time before giving it several light coats of lacquer for sealing. Some brass and copper were used in various places for a realistic appearance. Generally, ferrous material should not be used in static models; however, I feel that if sealed carefully it will last a long time. A solution of baking soda and water (pH 8.0) was used to neutralize acids in the wood, particularly where it came in contact with the steel. This also produced a weathering effect that I feel is safe – but time will be the judge of that.

The figurines were carved from one piece of holly and painted with acrylic paint.

There is a wealth of information in the US on inland waterways steamboats, ranging from books, plans and archives to well preserved photographs appearing in journals, which is readily available to the modeller sufficiently motivated to construct most types of US steamboat.

Bibliography

Bates, Allan L *The Western Rivers Steamboat Cyclopodium* (Hustle Press, Leona, N J, 1968)

Clemens, S L (Mark Twain) *Life on the Mississippi* (Harper & Brothers, New York, 1917)

Gandy, Joan & Thomas H *The Mississippi Steamboat Era* (Dover, New York, 1987)

Hanson, Joseph Mills *Conquest of the Missouri* (Rineheart & Co, New York, c1950)

Hunter, Louis C *Steamboats on the Western Rivers* (Harvard University Press, Cambridge, 1949)

Jackson, Donald *Voyages of the Steamboat Yellow Stone* (Ticknor & Fields, New York, 1985)

Way, Jr, Frederick *Way's Packet Directory 1848–1983* (Sons & Daughters of Pioneer Rivermen, Ohio University Press, Athens, Ohio, 1983)

Wiseman, William F 'Steamboat Indiana' (*Ships in Scale*, Model Expo, volume 3. 16–17–18)

Photographic Sources

Montana Historical Society, 225 North Roberts, Helena, Montana 59620–9990

Murphy Library, UW-La Crosse, WI 54601

The Public Library of Cincinnati and Hamilton County, 800 Vine Street, Library Square, Cincinnati, Ohio 54202–2071

Three views of the completed model. (*Photos by Gerald Thomas*).

Uncredited photographs are by the author

PILOT CUTTER

Garibaldi

by Dick Schipper

Colin Archer was a man of great repute in the sailing world. His ships – pilot boats and fishing boats – were much in demand among yachtsman in the first half of this century for their superb sailing qualities.

The son of a Scotsman who had emigrated to Norway, Archer was born in Larvik on 22 July 1832. After an education in Scotland he emigrated to Australia to join his brother. While still very young, he returned to Norway and took a job in a small shipyard in Jordfolden. He returned to Australia in 1850 and stayed there until 1861, after which he settled in Norway and began his career as a designer and builder of small boats.

In the nineteenth century pilot boats were relatively small and life aboard was harsh for the pilot and his crew, especially in winter. Pilots at that time tended also to be somewhat conservative in outlook, and Archer encountered considerable initial difficulty in persuading them to appreciate his work.

With Archer's designs, however, they soon found that they could stay longer at sea and could carry more sail, and thus could reach a ship before the competition, even in the worst weather conditions. The breakthrough came in a race for pilot boats at Arendal in 1886, in

which all of the first five to finish had been designed and built by Archer.

I chose to model the boat designed for Joseph Wilhelmsen in 1905, which he sailed under the name *Garibaldi*. The dimensions were as follows: length on deck 40ft 0in (12.20m), length on waterline 34ft 9in (10.60m), beam 13ft 9in (4.20m), draught 6ft 2in (1.85m), displacement 17 tons. She carried an external iron keel of 2 tons. The rest of the ballast was iron ore stowed in the bilges. She carried about 1075sq ft (100sq m) of canvas, and the mainsail had five rows of reefpoints and the jib three, so she could handle a wide variety of conditions.

This broadside view of the model gives a very good indication of the shape of the hull, particularly the underwater part.

Afloat, and just under way, the model looks very impressive.

Foredeck detail.

At first sight a Colin Archer design may appear to be rather tubby, but a look at the waterline plane shows a much slimmer shape. The broad upper end makes for a safe ship that rides the waves.

The model

Before determining the scale of a model, it is important to consider the waterline. A sailing model should have a waterline length upward of 3ft; a smaller model will simply not sail properly. The scale itself is important here: a sailing model one-tenth the size of the real ship will have a sail area only one-hundredth of the original, and will be one thousand times lighter. This naturally has a huge effect on sailing qualities. The smaller the scale the greater this difference becomes, so that a 4ft model of a ship at 1/50 scale will not sail as well as a similar sized model of a smaller ship at a scale of 1/10.

The model was built plank on frame at a scale of 1/10. The hull has seventeen planks to each side, and in its lower part there are two stealers at bow and stern. The planks were fastened to the frames by means of one nail and one treenail. For strength reasons the planks on the model run from bow to stern in one piece, but to suggest the use of shorter planks a cut was made into the plank and a thin layer of wood sliced off to one side.

The frames were made of plywood and the stem, stern and planking of ramin, which has a nice grain. A strip of black cardboard was placed in between the deck planks to suggest the caulked seams, and the whole hull was treated internally with epoxy resin and glass fibre tissue to ensure watertightness.

A ship that has been at sea for several years does not look as smooth as some of the highly finished models seen sailing nowadays; for true realism, a sailing model should look worn and battered. My sailing mate Joop Clobus built a model of the *Benjamin Latham* (a Grand Banks schooner) ten years ago, and after ten years of intensive sailing she looks better now than when she was new, simply because of wear and tear.

I have done everything in my power to prevent my model from having a polished look. The nails on deck were tipped with thin black paint, which was absorbed by the wood of the deck and gives the appearance of rusty nails. The unfinished model was then left outside in the sun to get a nice patina, after which the hull was given several coats of thin paint, which shows the grain of the wood nicely. The mast and spars were also made of ramin, and waxed rather than lacquered. All the metal parts were chemically blackened.

The sails

The sails were hand sewn (every stitch), as in the old days. I learned the original process aboard *Eendracht*, the Dutch National Sail Training Association vessel. I copied it on a small scale for the model, but the

Figure 1. Headsails
1. Earring lining
2. Sheet patch to above the position of the last reef point
3. Seam
4. Typical seam
5. Tack patch
6. Sheet patch

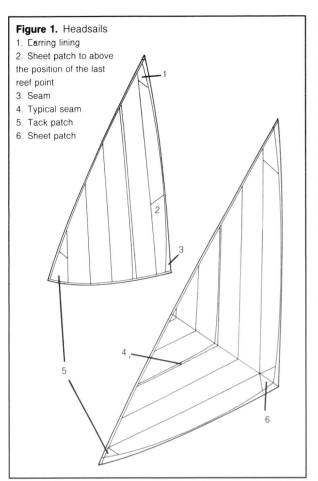

Figure 2. Mainsail
1. Earring lining
2. Typical seam
3. Seam
4. Half a cloth
5. Sheet patch
6. Foot

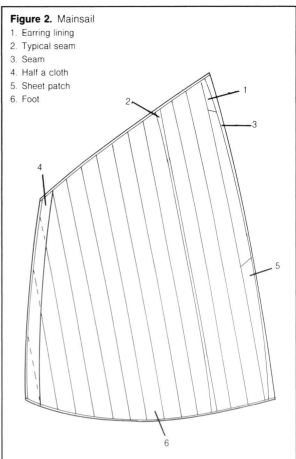

The after deck, showing the considerable beam of Colin Archer's design. *All photographs are by the author*

process is basically the same.

The width of the sail cloths varies in different countries (the Netherlands 74cm, England 24in or 61cm, and France 57cm). The cloths have an overlap of 1in (2.5cm), but towards the upper and lower leech this increases to 1½ to 2in (3.8 to 5.0cm) to produce the belly in the sail.

In model sailmaking working with cloths is difficult because the cotton has no selvedge of scale size; on the model, therefore, the overlap was imitated by folding. The cloth has to be stretched while sewing, and this was traditionally done by means of a sailhook. A model sailhook can be made out of a clothes peg with a small nail in one of the legs. For a right-handed modeller, this should be fastened to the right armrest of a chair. The needle should be held between thumb and forefinger and pushed through with the middle finger; it is best to use a long fine needle. Because all stitches are made the same way, all the yarns tend to twist, so it is important to untwist them from time to time in order to avoid knots or tangles.

Usually a sailmaker would start sewing on the fore leech but in model sailmaking it is easier to start on the after leech because of the selvedge. The fore and upper leeches are not cut straight, but in a slight curve (about ¼in per foot, or 1.5cm per metre) to produce the right belly. The fore leech is then doubled with a piece half a cloth wide. The foot in the lower leech is about 8 percent of its length.

After the sail has been finished it has to be leeched, and this has to be done very carefully. Note that in the fore leech the tension should be on the rope, while in the after leech the tension should be on the cloth and not on the rope. The best way to do this is to mark both sail and rope and to add or subtract rope as necessary.

Every self-respecting sailmaker will tell a different story about the exact measurements for leeching, so these figures need not be taken too

Right and opposite: These two views of the model sailing, one from the starboard bow and the other from the starboard quarter, show the full beauty of the design.

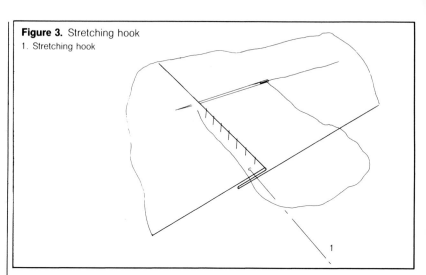

Figure 3. Stretching hook
1. Stretching hook

literally. There are numerous books on sailmaking which provide the necessary information, but there are also still some working sailmakers who can explain the traditional methods. I am lucky to have an acquaintance who rigged luggers in the first half of this century, and his successor still does work for museums.

Sailing the model

Because of its relatively large scale, the model is inherently stable, and will sail without an enlarged keel. Originally the keel was made of wood with a central core of iron, but in the model the scale keel can be removed and replaced by a solid lead keel weighing 15½lb (7kg). On a total weight of 37½lb (17kg) this gives adequate stability.

The model is controlled by three-function radio control, thus:
1. Rudder; this operates proportionally by means of a rope to the original tiller. The rudder has a plexiglas extension, though the model will sail without it, because in a strong breeze this gives better control.
2. Mainsail; this is controlled by a proportional sail winch, which pulls the end attached to the horse towards the mast.
3. Jib and flying jib; these are controlled by means of a messenger with end switches. The winch is attached to a speed control unit with forward and reverse and can be set very accurately.

On the transmitter the joystick controls operate thus: righthand, steer left/right; lefthand, mainsail (down is reeling in), jib and flying jib – stick to the left, sails to port; stick to the right, sails to starboard. There was no engine on board *Garibaldi*, and if she could do without one, so can I.

She is an excellent performer, both in running and manoeuvering, and sails well in winds up to Force 4. Those used to sailing M class yachts tend to pull the sails tight, but gaff rig needs some air, so it is best to ease off a bit on the sheets; after all, *Garibaldi* is not a racing machine.

All she has to do now is to weather down in sailing practice and acquire the look of a shaggy old boat!

HMS Tartar

(1734)

by Donald McNarry FRSA

The 20-gun Sixth Rate, single decked *Tartar* was built at Deptford Dockyard in 1734. Her gun deck length was 106ft, beam 30ft, and burden 420 tons. She saw service off the Florida coast in 1740 and in the East Indies between 1749 and 1751. She was broken up on the Thames in 1755.

The original dockyard model of the *Tartar*, to the somewhat unusual scale of 7ft = 1 inch, is at the National Maritime Museum, Greenwich, and is a most attractive item. It has the original rigging, and is one of the very few models of the 1700s to retain its original sails, though they

Starboard bow and port quarter views of the dockyard style model.

are somewhat the worse for the passing of close on 260 years. The boat is still on the booms, and the lower hull is partly planked, revealing single timbers, singly spaced.

When I photographed the model at Greenwich it was in an individual case and one could walk all round it examining and photographing it from every angle. This may still be so, but there is a tendency now for museums to rearrange matters so that galleries are ill-lit, and several models are grouped together in large brightly lit cases. This may or may not look attractive, and caters for the average visitor, but is unfortunate for the serious student if he wishes to study and photograph a particular model in detail.

There is apparently no Admiralty

This photograph gives a good idea of the deck layout of the vessel.

draught of the *Tartar*, but there are plans of two very similar vessels of the same dimensions, the *Sheerness* and the *Dolphin*. Both of these show sweep ports and I have included these though they are omitted from the original model.

The *Tartar* is shown here in two styles, a dockyard model with sails arranged slightly differently from the Greenwich model, and a waterline version with all sail set, but in a calm sea with her sweeps in operation. Both are to a scale of 16ft = 1in (1/192) and are 10½in long. They are in Yew cases.

Two quarter views of the *Tartar* with sweeps out.

On the waterline
model the deck is
shown fully planked.

The foredeck of the
dockyard style model.

*All photographs are by the
author*

THE ULLAPOOL
Post Boat

'DUNCAN THE POST'S BOAT'

by Hamish Barber

E ver eager to find a source of plans for old Scottish sailing craft, I read the small paragraph in *The Scotsman* with some anticipation. The information was brief: the owner of a small boat building yard in Lancaster had discovered the remains of a clinker built boat in a crofter's field near Ullapool in Ross and Cromarty, Scotland. It was said to be all that remained of the postboat – 'Duncan the Post's boat', as it was still remembered – that carried the mails from Ullapool over to the scattered community on the south side of

The finished model of 'Duncan the Post's Boat', 14in long overall.

Loch Broom, and further afield, round the headland to Little Loch Broom, from about the turn of the century until some time in the 1920s.

I had been building models of old Scottish fishing boats for some years, based on the excellent plans drawn in the 1930s by the late Philip Oke and now housed in the National Maritime Museum, but the supply of new plans was drying up. A newly discovered old boat with what must be a fascinating history was a very exciting prospect, and without delay I wrote to the newspaper and asked for the address of the Lancaster shipbuilders mentioned in the article.

The owner of Character Boats, of Overton Lancaster, could not have been more helpful. Almost by return of post came photographs of the remains of the boat, together with rough drawings of her likely lines (Figure 1). She was 14ft overall, transom sterned, with a maximum breadth of 6ft and a depth of 2¾ft amidships. The lines of prow and transom resembled those of a scaffie, with a deep raking forefoot and a sharply angled stern, and she boasted a 13½ft mast, set well forward, and a lug boom of 10ft. What made her so interesting was that she had a single dipping lug, and, knowing the job involved in tacking with such a sail, it seemed to me that Duncan the Post would probably have had to have been very careful to avoid that complicated and exhausting manoeuvre.

The first job was to draw the lines to 1/12 scale, quite a time-consuming prospect as the individual drawings on the rough plans I had received were not all to the same scale. That done, a building jig was constructed with one former cut to the hull lines a little aft of midships, and two further formers between the first and the bow, to preserve the beautiful curve of the forward aspect of the hull. The keel, forefoot and transom were cut from ¼in basswood and assembled together with the bow and stern deadwoods. The prow and the transom were left a couple of inches longer than required, to lift the model up in the building frame so that my rather over-sized fingers could get in to

Loch Broom Post Boat

14ft × 6ft × 1ft 4in
The original boat from which the lines of this GRP version were taken was used to deliver the mail on Loch Broom by 'Duncan the Post' about 60 years ago.

Original rig - dipping lug
Alternatives - standing lug and jib

Plan reproduced by kind permission of Mr Bailiff of Character Boats

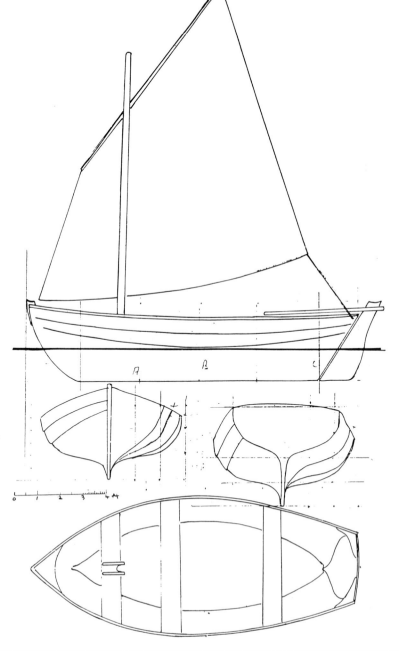

This photograph shows the internal construction, fittings and ancillary equipment of Duncan's boat.

fasten the final strake. For those not accustomed to the construction of a clinker built model, it must be explained that the hull is built upside down on the building frame, and lifted out only when all the strakes have been fitted.

The ten strakes each side were cut from $1/_{16}$in bass with the lands both glued and fastened with trenails of $1/_{32}$in diameter cut from bamboo cane. The breadth of the strakes had been marked on the sides of the formers and as the planking progressed I checked after each pair of strakes had been fitted to ensure that the beautiful sheer of the original boat was being reproduced. Once the last strake had been fastened the hull was taken out of the building jig and the stemhead and transom cut to the correct height.

A breasthook and transom knees were then shaped and fitted, and the extraordinary strength of such a light and seemingly fragile construction was finlly demonstrated when the inwale was installed, glued and dowelled. The timbers, running from the keel to the underside of the inwale, were of 3mm × 1½mm bass and positioned at ½in intervals, while three much more substantial

floors extended from the keel to the level of the deck. The fitting of the timbers completed, a stringer was attached ¾in down from the inwale, and the mast step was set on to the keel. Finally the inside of the boat was sanded down and coated with a dark brown paint.

The floorboards were effectively in three parts: the main, central, part was made as a separate unit and secured to the floors by the usual arrangement of a wooden spigot through a metal ring set in the floors and protruding through the planks. In such a boat, where some ballast was required – usually made up of boulders from the shore – it was necessary to ensure that the floorboards over the ballast could be lifted. The stern section was again made as an entity, fitting over the main section forward and the deadwood aft, and, as with the main section, this had to be removable to allow access for bailing the boat of rainwater or spray. Forward, a small reinforced raised platform was fitted, which, as with the other section of the flooring, was not secured to the hull.

The thwarts and their knees were made from ⅛in mahogany, unvarnished as they would be in life, and

secured to the stringer by bamboo dowels. The forward thwart carried a semicircular groove for the mast, reinforced with two strong vertical pieces extending aft and holed to take a metal post which formed the aft support for the raking mast. Between the metal post and the mast a shaped wedge ensured that the mast was held securely.

The mast and lug boom were made from ordinary hardwood dowel, shaped to give the correct taper. A curved piece was glued and dowelled to the yard at one third of its length to take the hook of the uphaul, while at the upper end of the mast a groove fitted with a sheave took the main halyard. Above the sheave I cut a recess in the mast to secure the Burton.

I derive an enormous amount of pleasure in fitting out the boats I build with what I know, or imagine, each would carry. The postboat had to have oars – a pair of 10ft sweeps with thole pins fitted just aft of the centre thwart – and a wooden scoop bailer, but as I sat and thought about this boat it seemed to me that there would be much else besides. The life of a rural postman, in the early years of this century, would not have been

– I thought – as busy and stressful as perhaps it is now. There would be plenty of time, and dependent as Duncan was on the wind and the tide, nobody could be sure just when he would arrive with the day's mail. This could be exploited, or perhaps 'used' would be a better word, so I decided that Duncan would probably find an opportunity to lay a lobster pot – and collect it a day or so later – and there would likely to a hand line on board for mackerel, or if the wind died, for a lazy hour or so fishing for haddock or cod.

The Postboat thus has a lobster pot on board, and a hand line, and a wooden rope-bound bucket. A thought then struck me. Raising a lobster pot is thirsty work, as is fishing for haddock in the flat calm of a summer day, so in the model Duncan has taken the precaution of filling the bucket with water . . . and you may just see in the photograph the neck of a bottle peeping out from the cool sea-loch water.

These four pictures show the remains of the Post Boat as found in a crofter's field near Ullapool, on the shores of Loch Broom. *By courtesy of Mr Bailiff of Character Boats*

Uncredited photographs are by the author

THE NAVAL
Gig

by Douglas Hamby

For a number of years the construction of clinker-built boats has engaged my attention as a necessary part of the equipment of larger models. They can, however, also be worthwhile models in their own right. The late Norman Ough produced a set of 1/48 scale drawings of warship boats to go with his highly detailed warship plans, and one of drawings, the 30ft gig, caught my eye. The gig shown in the Ough drawing is of the type in use in the

Looking aft, showing the fine bow lines.

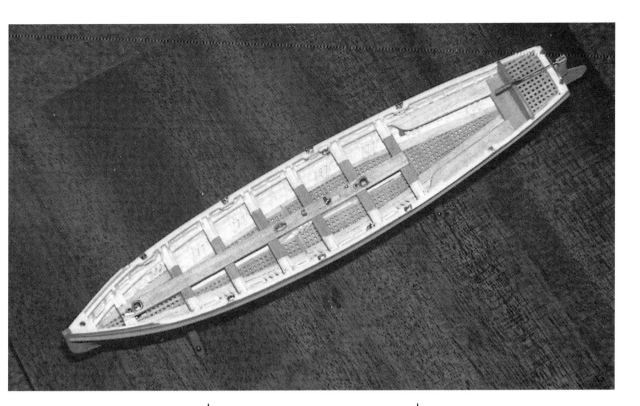

Royal Navy between the two World Wars. It was a slender craft, 30ft long, with three oars a side, single banked, with provision for four oars a side by fitting a portable thwart across the side benches. For sail propulsion it was equipped with dipping lugsails and could be either single or two-masted. A centreboard of ¼in thick galvanised steel plate could be lowered when sailing.

The plans show two forms of construction – double skin carvel and clinker. I have no information as to

This view shows the long narrow shape of the gig's hull, and the arrangement of thwarts and gratings.

A port quarter view; note the shape of the transom and rudder, and the sheet horse across the top of the transom.

The finished model, with masts and sails rigged.

The model
============

the relative popularity of the two systems and which, if either predominated.

The gig was the captain's personal boat, very smartly turned out and with a picked crew. I understand that larger warships would be issued with two gigs, one for the captain and the second for the executive commander. In this case the captain's boat would be known as the galley, probably a survival of nineteenth-century practice by which captains were issued with a galley for personal use.

With the coming of the internal combustion engine and the issuing of motor boats to ships, the gig fell into disuse; most captains preferred the motor boat. By 1935 we find the gig used by relatively junior officers for picnics and swimming parties, etc. The gig did not reappear in the post World War II Navy.

The model

The model is to 1/48 scale, and was built upside-down on a mould, in much the same way as is described in Harold Underhill's *Plank-on-Frame Models*, Volume II. The keel, hog, stem and transom are of boxwood. The slot for the centreboard was cut in the keel and a brass sole plate was necessary to provide much-needed stiffening, since the keel was unavoidably weakened by cutting the slot.

The hull is planked with sycamore veneer, sanded down from 0.025in to 0.019in, which is approximately scale size. Before commencing planking, I prepared a table of girths so that the plank taper at the ends could be measured accurately. The edge of each plank (which provides the land for the next) had to be bevelled to prevent the planks springing away from the mould as the work pro

ceeded. When the planking was complete up to the gunwale, the rubbing strakes and bilge rails were fitted before the boat was removed from the mould. A cradle was made to receive it before doing this, as such hulls are very frail at this stage.

When the hull was removed from the mould a $1/32$in square strip of boxwood stringing was fitted inside and at the top of the gunwale strake on each side. The timbers, which went in next, were spaced $3/16$in apart, and were made from $1/32$in strips of lime veneer. They butt closely against the hog, and were 'sprung' into place under the gunwale. Some heat was necessary to bend them to the required radius without snapping.

The centreboard case was made up from two panels of 1mm ply separ-

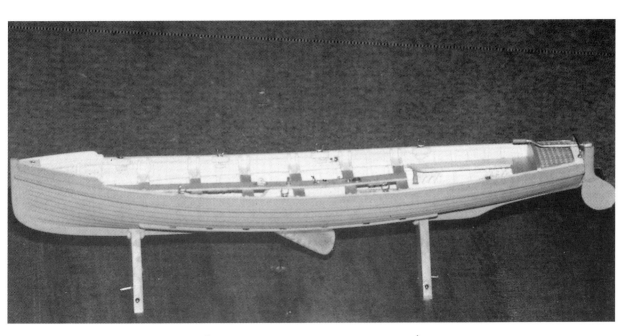

The centreboard partly lowered.
All photographs are by Mike Higginbottom

ated by a spacer along the sides and top, so that the centreboard could be housed. The panels were then fitted in a limewood frame. An open slot was left in the top of the casing for the lever used to raise and lower the centreboard. The casing was then glued to the hog.

The floors were fitted next. They were cut from $1/16$in sycamore. The upper surface of the floor is level and the lower side is shaped to fit the curve of the timbers. The outer ends of the floors were used to mark the position of the bilge stringer, a $1/16$in boxwood strip running the length of the boat on either side. It acts as margin plank for the gratings and a landing for the lower edge of the stretcher supports. The gratings were made up in batches, six in all. The grating material was cut by hand in a jig, and slotted for fully halved joints from $1/32$in square boxwood strip.

The stretcher supports were made up from boxwood strip assembled in a jig, and then fitted into the boat with their lower ends glued to the bilge stringer. The mast steps were also fitted at this stage. The risings to support the thwarts were fitted next. These are of $1/32$in square boxwood strip, and are in two sections, one for the main thwarts and the other for the stern benches.

The thwarts were made from $1/32$in lime, but before they were fitted two eyebolts had to be fitted just forward of the mast steps to take the hallards. The thwarts were then fitted and the thwart knees, of boxwood (four knees per thwart). The side and stern benches were made from lime and the stern bench backrest from a piece of light brown wood. Under each thwart amidships is a turned wood stanchion, and there is also one at the end of each side bench.

There is a mast carling running fore and aft on the top of the thwarts, its top surfaces fitted with eyebolts, eyeplates, mast sockets etc in brass. Under the board are wooden cleats for securing the running rigging.

The gunwale was capped with sycamore veneer, and fitted with a short washboard at the bow. Brass plates, drilled to take the rowlocks, were fitted to the top of the capping rail. Provision is made for eight rowlocks, but only six were fitted. The rudder was made from a very thin piece of boxwood with pads glued to each side of the stock. The hinges were bent up from copper shim. The tiller was made from brass with a turned wooden grip fitted to it. The space between the stern bench backrest and transom was closed with at grating. A brass sheet horse was fitted to the transom.

The centreboard was then fitted permanently, with the operating lever threaded through the top of casing. Once in position, the handle for the lever was soldered in place.

The inside of the boat was painted white (Humbrol satin finish). The thwarts, gratings etc were given two coats of Ronseal matt varnish. The outside of the hull was painted a medium grey.

The masts and spars were turned from lancewood. The masts have a brass cap which was drilled through to form a dummy sheave for the halliards. The sails were made from tracing linen after the size had been boiled out. All seams, linings, tablings and reef bands were represented by strips of white airmail paper, secured in place with fabric glue. The roping round the sail edge (always on the port side of a fore and aft sail) was also glued on. (I am indebted to fellow modelmaker David Gabbutt for the method of sailmaking, which he used to great effect on his model of the Swedish Royal Yacht *Amphion*.

All loose gear, such as oars, stretchers, boat hooks etc was left off the model so that the internal construction details were not obscured. In practice the gig would have been equipped with four 17ft oars and two 16ft oars.

HMS Diana (1794)

Details of the 1/192 scale 38-gun frigate featured on this issue's front cover

by Philip Reed

dalised'. The main topgallant and royal sheets are eased to allow the wind to fill the sails, and the fore topsail is partly becalmed by the main. The fore topmast staysail is set to help throw the head off the wind in the event of a sudden yaw, or shift of wind forward, but is, of course, at present also becalmed. The case is veneered with walnut burr.

Diana was built at Rotherhithe on the Thames by Randall and Brent, launched in March 1794, and fitted out in the Royal Dockyard at

The completed model.

When I built my first ship model some twenty years ago one of my biggest problems was to find accurate and authentic information about the ships I wanted to build. The situation is very different today. My particular interest for several years has been the ships of the Napoleonic era, for which nowadays there is a wealth of information readily available in the works of authors such as Brian Lavery, Peter Goodwin, James Lees, and in Conway's *Anatomy of the Ship* series of in-depth studies of individual ships. Also, quite indispensable in my opinion – particularly for the maker of waterline models – is John Harland's *Seamanship in the Age of Sail*.

My model of *Diana* is to a scale of 1/16in = 1ft (1/192), and was built almost wholly in accordance with the information given in *The Frigate Diana* by David White, a volume in the Anatomy of the Ship series. I did, however, come across a few minor differences in some matters pertaining to rigging, in particular relating to the lead of ropes, between this book and the James Lees' *The Masting & Rigging of English Ships of War 1625-1860*.

She is depicted in a relatively calm sea with a freshening wind on the quarter, almost astern. The mizzen royal has been furled and stowed in the topmast shrouds, the topgallant is furled, and the topsail 'scan-

This port quarter view shows the impressive amount of sail carried.

Diana's bow.

Deptford. She had a length on the gun deck of 146ft 3in, extreme breadth of 38ft 3½in, and depth in hold of 13ft 9in. Armament comprised twenty-eight 18pdr and ten 9pdr carriage guns, plus six carronades. She had a busy and successful career, and was eventually sold to the Dutch Government in 1815, being lost by fire when in drydock in Willemsoord in January 1839.

The figurehead, before the bowsprit was fitted.

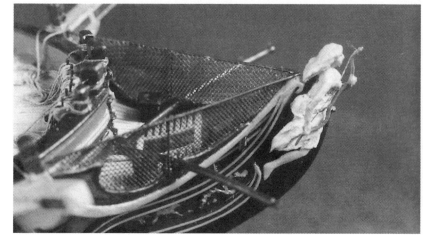

A good view of the detail required on the upper deck, before the forecastle and quarterdecks were fitted.

The midship area of the model.

References

Peter Goodwin *The Construction and Fitting of the Sailing Man of War 1650-2850*, Conway Maritime Press Ltd, London, 1987.

John Harland *Seamanship in the Age of Sail*, Conway Maritime Press Ltd, London, 1984.

Brian Lavery *The Arming & Fitting of English Ships of War 1600-1815*, Conway Maritime Press Ltd, London, 1987.

James Lees *The Masting & Rigging of English Ships of War 1625-1860*, Conway Maritime Press Ltd, London, 1979 & 1984.

David White *The Frigate Diana*, Conway Maritime Press Ltd, London, 1987. ❑

(Left) The ship's outfit of boats included a 32ft pinnace, 26ft launch, two 24ft cutters and an 18ft cutter or jolly boat.

The quarterdeck, showing the wheel, binnacle, capstan, etc.

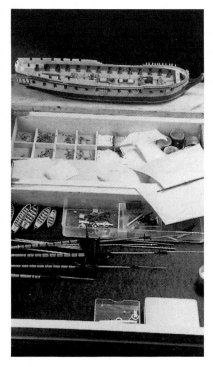

This view of the model under construction gives a good idea of some of the many component parts required.

The mainmast and some of its rigging.

All photographs are by the author

The Udenmää *Gamla*

A Swedish skerry frigate of 1760

by A Ludbrook

that Russia was Sweden's superior at sea because she possessed a special galley fleet for operations in confined waters. He went on to say that the whole of Finland, then a Swedish possession, would be lost if Russia gained control of the Finnish coast. Loewen's ideas had considerable influence on future Swedish defence plans.

Sweden fought Russia again in 1741 with little success, and in 1747 the Swedish Admiralty sent Lieutenants Rajalin and Kullen-

In 1720, at the battle of Ledsund, a large Russian galley fleet overwhelmed four Swedish frigates. The Swedish Admiral Sjöblad was court-marshalled and had to forfeit a year's pay. Although the Russians had suffered severe losses in the battle Sweden was very impressed by the performance of the Russian galleys and drew up plans for a considerable inshore fleet. However, at that time Sweden was suffering an economic depression and was unable to implement these plans.

In 1723 Major General Loewen reported to the Swedish Admiralty

Two views of the hull of the model under construction.

Looking aft from the port bow.

The after deck; note the shape of the tiller.

berg to study the galley fleets of France, Genoa and Malta. They reported in 1750, and pointed out that the Mediterranean countries possessed a human resource that Sweden lacked, namely a large population to use as galley oarsmen. In 1756 the Swedish inshore fleet was reorganised and became a branch of the Army, remaining

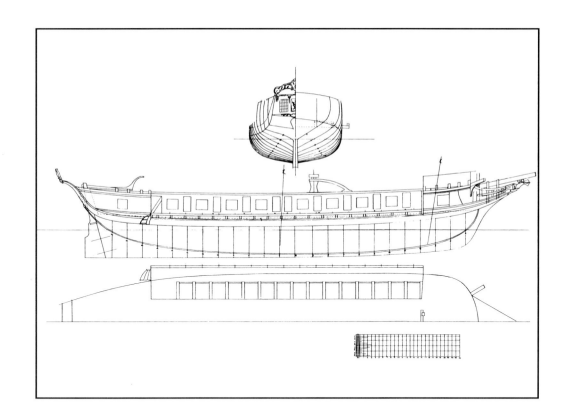

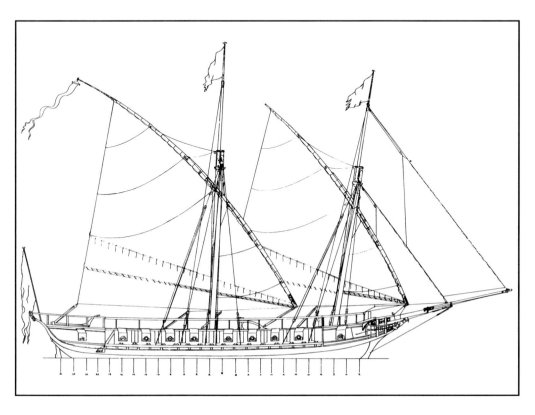

Above: note the guns ranged along the centreline. Since the capstan spindle could not pass through the battery it was supported by a curved strongback.

appointed Shipwright at Stralsund in Swedish Pomerania (now Germany). Chapman reported to General Augustin Ehrensvärd, the military commander of Sweden's continental provinces, who was responsible for constructing the Sveaborg fortress near Helsinki and for the creation of a new inshore fleet. This fleet was intended to operate in the skerries, the rocky islands along the shores of Sweden and Finland which formed a natural barrier along the most populated regions of both countries.

At first only galleys similar to those in the Russian navy were considered for the new fleet, but as a result of experience gained in oper-

under its control until 1813.

During the years 1759-62 Sweden was again at war, this time with Prussia. In 1760 the famous naval architect F H Chapman was

This design of stern, with the main wales sweeping up on either side of the transom, was typical of many of Chapman's ships.

ations on the coast of Pomerania in 1759 the building of the galleys was abandoned and alternative designs were considered.

When Chapman and Ehrensvärd heard in 1760 that Russia was starting to build warships modelled on the Mediterranean xebec they both agreed that this was not a suitable craft for Swedish use as it required a large skilled crew to handle the lateen sails. To combat the growing Russian threat Chapman was asked to design heavily armed ships suitable for operations in the confined waters of the skerries. These were to be capable of being sailed, rowed and fought by small crews.

He designed four types of skerry frigate, each type being named after a Finnish province (the spelling of these ship types varies from source to source, depending on whether Swedish or Finnish spelling is used). The Turunmää was a shallow draught vessel with one gun deck. Her oars worked on crutches on a narrow outrigger above the main deck guns. The Hemeenmää was a larger version of the Turunmää with the oars worked in pairs between the gunports. The Pohjanmää was a ketch-rigged gunboat with a pair of 24pdrs at bow and stern. The Udenmää, of which the *Gamla* was the first, was the most revolutionary and least successful.

The *Gamla* was 102ft between perpendiculars and had a draught of 5ft (these are Swedish feet, equal to 296mm or 11.65 inches). She was armed with ten 12pdrs and two 3pdrs. Two of the 12pdrs were forward under the forecastle, and the two 3pdrs aft. These guns were mounted on normal gun carriages. The remaining 12pdrs were mounted on traversing carriages along the centreline. The original drawings also show small cannon mounted on the spar deck, but these are not listed as fitted, and would have overburdened such a shallow draught vessel. The rig was in the form of split lateen, in which the equivalent of a jib and gaff sail were set from a lateen yard. This was an attempt to achieve the advantages of a lateen rig without the requirement for a large crew. In the normal lateen rig a large crew is required, especially during tacking, when the lateen yard is passed round the mast.

Contemporary paintings also show square topsails set flying on the topmasts. This rig did not prove very successful, and was only in use for a period of some 30 years, after which it was replaced by a polacre barque rig. Oar benches were pro-

The finished model.

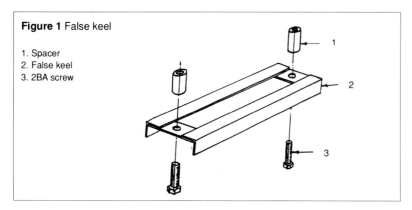

Figure 1 False keel

1. Spacer
2. False keel
3. 2BA screw

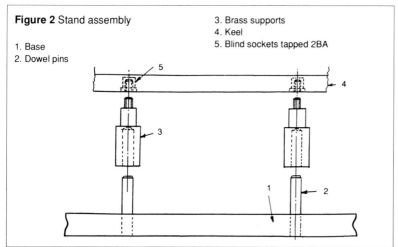

Figure 2 Stand assembly

1. Base
2. Dowel pins

3. Brass supports
4. Keel
5. Blind sockets tapped 2BA

vided on each side of the central battery, with doors between the gunports for the oarsmen.

Only three Udenmääs were built, the *Gamla* in 1760, the *Thorborg* in 1772, and the *Ingrebord* in 1776. The *Thorborg* was a larger version of the *Gamla*, with the split lateen rig replaced by a simplified square rig. The *Ingrebord* dispensed with the deck over the battery.

There was another vessel of the same name, also built in 1760, but she was a Pohjanmää. The two are often differentiated by being referred to as the *Udenmää Gamla* and the *Pohjanmää Gamla*. The latter was lost in 1775, but the *Udenmää Gamla* lasted a long time, as she took part in the battle of Svenskund in 1789 (see *Naval wars in the Baltic* by R C Anderson, page 261).

Research

Like most ship modellers I am always on the lookout for suitable subjects. I decided to build a model of *Gamla* after several years spent putting aside information about completely different vessels. For a long time I had thought about building a sailing model of a lateen rigged vessel, but hesitated because of the difficulties involved in tacking, when in theory the yard should be passed round in front of the mast.

However, browsing through Bjorn Landstrom's book *The Ship* I came across a drawing on page 183, figure 421 (1), of a ship with a split lateen rig. This I stored away in my mind as a possible future model. Later I obtained a copy of a draught which appeared to be of the same vessel. This is also to be

found on page 32 of the book *F H Chapman* by D G Harris. I believe these drawings represent the Hemeenmää *Oden*, a painting of which is reproduced on page 144 of Harris' book.

In 1985 I visited the Sea Finland Exhibition at Greenwich, hoping to find out more about the *Oden*. On display was a large model of the Udenmää *Thorborg*, and the hull struck me as being both interesting and attractive, although her looks were ruined by the stumpy square rig. However, the accompanying notes stated that she had been lateen rigged originally. Since detailed drawings of the *Thorborg* had been published in *The Man of War* by Macintyre and Bathe, page 34 figure 3, I decided that this was the ship to model; all I needed was a rigging plan. I wrote to the Swedish Maritime Museum in Stockholm. They were extremely helpful, and replied that they had no records showing the *Thorborg* as anything but square rigged, but that they had both a small and a large Udenmää with lateen rig. I purchased both sets at a very reasonable price.

The large Udenmää was a very attractive vessel, but my sources indicated that she was never built. The same sources stated that the drawings for the small Udenmää represented the *Gamla*, and by using the inboard details available for the *Thorborg* I felt I had enough information to produce reasonably detailed plans (Figures 1 and 2). The details of the traversing cannon were taken from plates in Chapman's *Architectura Navalis Mercatoria*. The major difference between the *Thorborg* and the *Gamla*, apart from size and rig, was that the former had hinged bulwarks which were lowered outboard when rowing to act as supports for the oars.

The model

The scale of the model is 1/35. It

has the following dimensions:

Length from taffrail to tip of figurehead: 41in (104cm)
Length overall: 53in (135cm)
Height from keel to truck: 35in (89cm)
Beam over rowing frame: 10in (25cm)
Weight: 6lb (2.72kg); *weight of add-on keel*: 4lb (1.8kg)

The model was built in the conventional manner with plywood frames erected on a ramin keel. The hull was planked in lime. I found it quite difficult to plank the bluff shallow bow, and some of the planks finished up being nearly S shaped. The yards and masts are of ramin. The yards were curved by soaking them in household ammonia, bending them to shape on a jig, and allowing them to dry. The sails are of boiled draughting linen.

Two views of the model afloat; note the split lateen rig.

All photographs are by the author

The model has had her first sailing trials but these were not completely successful, and further work needs to be done on the design of the additional keel. The present false keel was fabricated from two lengths of steel angle, so that the model can stand upright when being prepared for a sail (see Figure 1). The model was fitted with two blind brass sockets tapped 2BA and securely Araldited into the keel. The brass supporting stands screwed into these. The bottoms of these brass stands were drilled with 8mm holes and located on to two 8mm studs Araldited to the display case (see Figure 2). To fit the false keel the model is lifted off the baseboard, the two brass stands are unscrewed, and the false keel fitted using 2BA bolts and spacers, as in Figure 1. For sailing the scale sheets are replaced by a continuous line rove through eyebolts on the deck. At present only rudder controls have been fitted, although there is provision for a sail winch. However, I have not yet found a way to rig this without destroying the scale appearance.

Finally, a word of caution, often stated but well worth repeating. Do work out the final overall size of the intended model before starting work on it. I did not draw out my rigging plan to finished model size, and now have a model which is inconvenient to transport and too large to display in the house!

Sources

Statens Sjohistoriska Museum, Stockholm: original drawings of the small Udenmää.
*Svenska Flottans Historia** by G Haldin (Malmo 1943)
Architectura Navalis Mercatoria by F H Chapman
F H Chapman by Daniel G Harris (Conway, London 1990)
Oared Fighting Ships by R C Anderson (Percival Marshall, London 1962)
*The Mariner's Mirror** Volume for 1913, Articles by Rear Admiral J Hagg
*Copies of these works are in the Science Museum library, South Kensington, London SW7 5NH

I have spent the last ten years or so building four Victorian battleships: *Devastation, Empress of India*, (*Royal Sovereign* class), the ill-fated *Victoria* and finally *Magnificent* (*Majestic* class). I have done other minor jobs as well, but the main effort has been directed at these four.

Looking for something different to model I decided on HMS *Belfast* (1939) which had the appeal of being extant. In addition, there is an 'Anatomy of the Ship' volume devoted to the vessel; and friends supplied me with further photographs and plans.

I decided on a scale of 1/150. This resulted in a model 49½in long which is reasonable for carriage and display. I would like to build bigger but storage is a problem.

Using Perspex

My last few models have seen an increase in the use of Perspex. I find this a near perfect material for my kind of work. It produces very clean cut shapes, gives a perfect painting surface, glues well, particularly with cyanoacrylate, and can be machined with normal drills and cutters. One great advantage over metal is the ease with which small holes can be drilled. With the sort of model I build, large numbers of holes, down to about 0.012in diameter, are required. Drilling these in brass work is difficult and very frustrating, particularly if you break a drill.

In normal engineering most holes are only one or two diameters deep. With Perspex models the thickness of sheet used often means holes are required many diameters deep. In these cases the drill needs to be lubricated with water to avoid it simply jamming itself in its own hole. In addition, you should not force the drill in quickly, but relieve the pressure frequently and get rid of the swarf at short intervals. If those precautions are taken the task is fairly easy.

Gluing with epoxy (Araldite) is only partially successful and really only suitable for joints that are low stressed. The best adhesive is cyano which is also good for joining brass and Perspex though the speed with which it does can be a problem. The adhesive needs to be applied, therefore, with the pieces pre-positioned. An even better technique is to feed the adhesive in from the back. For instance, if a door (brass etching) is to be fixed to the side of a structure, drill three holes through the side behind the door. Fix the door with drafting tape in the correct position and then from the other side feed in

The completed model.

The bridge, port side. This has been sprayed. Note the masked ports and marked out position for the light. The drilled holes on the front face are for hand and foot rails.

way as wood when making super-structure units. Normally, I cut four sides and a top, the top being used to keep the sides square by being inset; two of the sides overlap the other two, and I use a disc sander to clean up the corners. (This is a most useful tool for this type of work as long as it has a table and right-angle lay.) It is best not to fit a base as this precludes access to the inside, which is often desirable. However, sometimes a partial base is useful for fixing securing dowels and the like. I always inset this about a millimetre so that it will not interfere with shaping the lower edge of the structure to suit deck camber.

I find it is useful to dowel everything, if at all possible, as this gives positive and, when glued, permanent positioning.

the cyano through the holes. You will be able to see the fluid run into the joint. In this way excess cyano should not get on the front surface.

Perspex can be used in the same

Assembly under way. Note the absence of gun barrels mentioned in the text.

The front of the crane mechanism assembly. This has three motors and gearboxes – slewing, raising jib, and load lifting.

Always remember that acrylic sheet is cast and not calendered (rolled) like poly sheet, and is therefore more rigid than poly but more brittle. I think the minimum thickness, with Perspex anyway, is 1mm. It can be sawn thinner but you need the equipment and some skill to do that. The faces of the original casting mould are of glass which imparts a very high surface gloss which is useless for most model work. Just flat it with glass paper or wet and dry, used dry, please. If you do this before assembly you can use a pencil for marking out.

Small items can be made solid and thin sections can be glued together to make suitably-sized chunks. Band saws and circular saws (fine teeth) cut acrylic well; most power fretsaws do not for the cut gets welded up by the hot blade. Hand fretsaws, however, work well. I find very fine metal cutting blades work efficiently on thin sheet. Thicker pieces can be cut using a coarser blade, but these will shatter thin sections. If you have shatter trouble with thin sheet, then saw it together with a hardboard or ply backing.

One advantage of using transparent acrylic is that ports can be machined directly into the plastic using a slot drill. All that is needed is to machine a flat bottomed recess of the diameter of the port about 0.005in deep. This needs a disc of masking tape to protect it before spraying. I made up a punch and die to punch out the discs.

Etching

Since my introduction to photo-etching each succeeding model has incorporated ever more etched parts. On *Belfast* nearly all the metal parts are in photo-etched 0.004in brass. At 1/150 scale this represents a thickness of 0.6in. Where thicker parts are required I have glued or soldered two 0.004in etchings together. The standard dished steel door is an example.

Using etched material involves a complete rethink of the fabrication process. Most of the real work lies not on the bench, as in normal practice, but on the drawing board – in many ways even before the drawing board. In my article in *MS 88* I explain the process of photo-etching in detail.

The hull

Hull construction employed the bread-and-butter principle, using jelutong. I laid the after deck in close-grained pine. The scale width of the planks is 0.07in, which corresponds to the width of planks in *Belfast*'s present deck, which was relaid fairly recently.

The fore main director. The piece of card behind the ladder is for its protection. To give an idea of size, the rectangular aerial opening is 30mm x 5mm. Note the 'open' breakwater door, lower left.

The forward deck, forward of the breakwater, is bare steel with three lines of weld put down in a 16in square pattern. To scale these three lines had to be represented as one. Unfortunately, the welds do not meet at the corners, so drawing the artwork was a nightmare – a great number of lines ¼in long. I found that I could only work for about ten minutes at a time. However, the resulting custom surface etched 0.007in brass deck was well worth the effort. I scribed the plate joins after toying

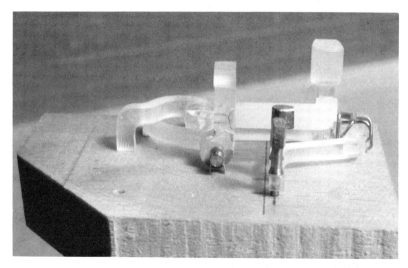

Elaborate ducting – a total of three motors and fans. I find it best to construct such sub-assemblies on a building board before transferring them to the model.

with, and rejecting, the idea of laying separate plates. It is always difficult to find the balance between absolute correctness and that which will look right. It is all to easy to fall into the trap of making the work look over fussy, especially when working to a scale of 1/150. With very small scales simulation can frequently produce better results than a poor attempt at slavish correctness.

On the other hand the desired result can often be obtained by simply doing what was done originally. The knuckle line on *Belfast*'s bow was a case in point. This is a rather subtle feature which is taken for granted unless it is done badly, whereupon it becomes the proverbial sore thumb. The line is produced by two surfaces coming together. The snag is that the angle between the two planes is not great and it becomes difficult to produce a clean line – it is either lost or shifts about vertically. I tried to produce it by carving, only to arrive at the result so often seen on other models: a poorly defined wavy line (one not likely to impress the judges). I decided to see how it was done on the ship. It was easy. The top plate was made to overhang the ver-

The intricate foremast assembly. Radar aerials have not yet been fitted.

The finished bridge. The four vertical cylinders on the bridge are Type 274 lookout sights. The bridge wind deflectors are etched as one piece, so no soldering is required. The same applies to the handrails. The Union Flag on B turret was sprayed on to a piece of 0.005in Plasticard.

tical curve of the lower part, thus making a nice angle into which the weld could be run. So I plated the top area lying between the deck and the knuckle, letting it slightly overlap the flared lower part. This plate could be shaped accurately before fitting, thus automatically building in the knuckle.

Another piece of research concerned the various outlets along the side of the hull. As built these were 'piped' down to the waterline to avoid stains on the hull paintwork. Most, if not all of these square section 'pipes' had been lost or removed. In many

instances it took a powerful glass to differentiate between a pipe and a stain. On the model the pipes are made of Perspex and follow the contour of the hull, ie, over the armour. At the upper end a top hat section closed and secured the pipe. I made up a press tool to form these from brass shim.

Another problem on the hull lay with the armour belt, and the bulge which was added during the repairs following the extensive damage caused by the mine in 1939. This required a number of pieces to be secured to the outside of the hull. Plasticard was my first choice, but this I rejected as I am not keen on long glued joints of different materials. I am always concerned that, when subject to fluctuations in temperature, their different rates of expansion and contraction will eventually crack the joint and ruin that time-

consuming paint finish. In the end I used ply and wood for the job.

Masts and radars

There were a number of particularly difficult parts to model, and these are worth considering in detail. Probably the most striking feature of *Belfast* after the 1959 refit was the elaborate mast structure designed to support the ever more advanced electronic arrays. Both masts were four-sided tapered columns based on four-cornered round-sectioned tubes. I decided to make four etchings, one for each face containing all the horizontal members as well as the diagonal struts. This meant the basic mast consisted of four wires (the corner columns) and four appliqued etchings. I thought these would be simple to assemble as the etchings would space the corner wires. In the event I had to make up a fixture to support the

Starboard side of the bridge.

wires and the etchings in their correct positions before attempting to solder them together. If I did the job again I would etch the four sides as one, folding them up on assembly. With etched parts, unless there are other reasons for not so doing, it is best to have as few joints as possible. Joints mean alignment problems which are totally eliminated if drawn as a whole.

With the main structure complete, the interior horizontal cross members could be soldered in. These produce rigidity in the structure. The only problem here was preventing the last one falling out when soldering in the next one. This was avoided by using ladies' two-prong curl clips (plain) as heat shunts. I managed to persuade my wife's hairdresser to buy me a box of seventy-two when

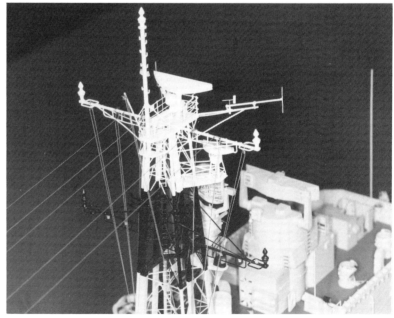

Foremast detail. Note the weather vane on the starboard side and the foot rests on the pole mast supporting the dunce's hat of the type AJE aerial outfit.

she went to the wholesaler. They are extremely useful for all sorts of jobs as you can bend the twin prongs or cut them short or remove just one to do whatever you want. I find them even more useful than the ubiquitous spring clothes peg.

Before attaching the masts to the model there were sundry items such as ladders, radar wave guides and cables to be fitted. These were best slid in from the bottom. The wave guides I made from Perspex strip. Those peculiar conical dunce-hat aerials of the type AJE outfit I form turned – the first time I had attempted to make these.

The fighting lights I turned from Perspex but nearly everything else was etched including the double curved dish of the type 277Q radar and the foot 'ropes' on the yards which on *Belfast* were made of steel.

Eight controlled-range, blind fire directors were required. They controlled the 4in secondary armament and the twin Bofors. Many modellers avoid making these by suggesting them under their 'pram' covers. Basically, they are a tub with an out-turned top edge. However, their outer

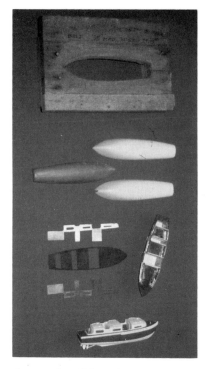

Construction of the 35ft medium-speed motor boat. From top: female mould; male mould (left) with, right, two hull mouldings in 0.020in white poly sheet; a set of etched cabin parts with, right, the etched parts soldered together; a completed and painted boat.

vertical surface is covered with detail; doors, hatches, ladders and reinforcing ribs. Their interiors are a nightmare and quite impossible for me to model accurately at 1/150 scale. Here it really is a matter of simulation rather than replication. This might be possible if one had a complete set of drawings but even after making sketches from them on *Belfast* herself I decided against it.

To put the exterior detail on the tub was quite simple. A development in 0.004in brass was etched and simply rolled round a pre-turned tub

Boat stowage aft of the bridge. It is always difficult to ascertain the outfit of boats at any given time. Here two 35ft medium-speed boats are on the platform, with the crane jib housed between them. The two seaboats are 27ft motor whalers (outboard with life ropes). Inboard of the whaler is a 36ft motor and pulling pinnace, and nestling under the crane jib is a 25ft motor cutter. A 27ft pulling whaler is stowed on the deck. There are some minor differences between the two 35ft medium speed boats. Note the lagged exhaust pipe on the after end of the bridge.

machined with its walls as thin as possible.

I broke down the interior into a series of shaped Perspex blocks, not forgetting the seats. The type 262 radar dish was turned with a spigot on the reverse to fit it into its housing. The inside faces were strewn with little pieces of plastic to simulate switch boxes etc. These together with bits of wire completed the job. Some details were painted on.

Main armament turrets

These were machined from solid rectangular chunks of Perspex. The holes for a gun's barrels and central pivot were first drilled with the block standing vertically. With the block laid down on to a rotary table, located by the pivot hole, all the vertical faces, including the rear radial face, were vertically milled with the machine head angled over where necessary. The turrets were completed by milling the compound angled tops. The main problem was clamping the block to the rotary table. The clamps had to be continually moved to allow the cutting to proceed.

I had drilled the gun barrel holes parallel with the turret base, *ie* horizontally. When I assembled the turrets and barrels the result looked very poor, with the barrels appearing to droop. I also made another mistake and that was not assembling barrels to turrets before putting the assembly on the model. I fixed the turrets to their barbettes without the guns as I thought the barrels would be a hazard when rigging; the threads being likely to get caught up. With the turrets fixed I could do little to correct the barrel holes which should have been drilled at a slight angle to

The area round the base of the mainmast. Note the two rectangular mesh cages for the aerials as well as the two vertical aerial protection cylinders, and the wood stowed in the timber store on top of the 4in gun crew's shelter.

give the guns an aggressive look. It then occurred to me that if the holes could not be altered, the barrels, although already sprayed and finished, could be.

As can be seen from Figure 1a, by reducing the diameter of the fixing spigot by a given amount the barrel could be fixed with Araldite with a 3 degree upward slope. Luckily, I had made the spigot longer than it need have been.

For the mathematically minded, the diameter to which the spigot must be reduced can be calculated by solv-

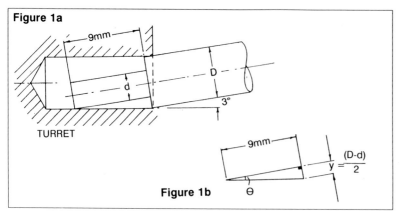

Figure 1a

9mm

D

d

3°

TURRET

9mm

$y = \frac{(D-d)}{2}$

θ

Figure 1b

ing the right-angled triangle shown in Figure 2. If the barrel is to be inclined at 3°, that is θ = 3°, and the length of the spigot is to be 9mm, then the reduction in *radius* will be: (D-d) ÷ 2 or $\frac{(D-d)}{2}$. For simplicity call this y.

Now $y/_9$ = tan θ, or y = 9 tan 3 (where θ = 3°).

From a table of natural tangents, we find that the tangent for 3° is 0.0524. Therefore y = 9 x 0.0524 =

0.472mm. Thus the diameter of the original spigot in this example will have to be reduced by 2 x 0.472mm or 0.944mm.

By fitting the turrets without the barrels I found it difficult to line them up. It would have been much easier to have assembled them beforehand on a surface plate with blocks. I made up a U-shaped piece of wire to fit into the muzzle to keep the barrels parallel.

Twin Bofor turrets

I spent a long time collecting photographs and plans of these installations before drawing out four views. The main parts were etched which included surface etching detail on the outside. It was possible to etch the deflection sights together with the cooling pipes. There was a lot of detail under the platform which I added although at the time it was difficult to decide whether any of it would show on the assembly.

Life raft stowages

There were well over twenty of these to be made so some sort of mass production was called for. They were made with the canvas covers fitted as they are always shown thus. What I

The after superstructure forward of X turret. The octagonal structure just forward of the main director is the emergency conning position over the ready use AA ammunition stowage.

The two forward MkV twin 40mm Bofors mountings either side of the controlled blind fire director. The ready use ammunition lockers are behind, against the side of the bridge structure. Note the rectangular aerial trunk above the lockers. Below are the white canvas covers of the inflatable life raft stowages. To give some indication of size, the diameter of the director is $^5/_8$in (16mm).

wanted to do was to carve three units in wood, all slightly different, as they were canvas remember, and then make silicon rubber moulds of these, prior to casting the rafts in Isopon. In the event I did not have any silicon rubber so I made one mould from styrene sheet instead.

The base of the raft stowage assembly was a 0.007in brass rectangle somewhat smaller than the finished overall size of the unit. A simple plate jig was made to drill five holes; four for the legs and one for the hydro-

static release valve. Using the jig, five holes were drilled into a piece of scrap wood to make a soldering fixture. About 120 short pieces of 0.5mm wire were bent into a right angle.

Figure 2

1. Profile of cast Isopon
2. 0.007in brass sheet
3. Four legs
4. Cut off hydrostatic valve to correct length

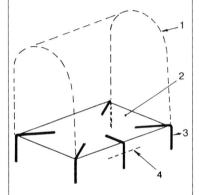

Five pieces of wire and one brass plate were assembled in the jig as shown in Figure 2 and soldered up. I was going to make the four legs from two U-shaped pieces but that would have required accuracy in bending up to get the correct spacing between the legs, and I try to make things as simple as possible.

The mould was then sprayed with release agent and filled with Isopon, making sure any air spaces/bubbles were eliminated. The leg assembly previously made was then pushed into the Isopon in the correct position with any excess Isopon scraped off. When set, the legs provided a means of prising the component out of the mould. The piece of brass representing the hydrostatic release was trimmed off to the correct length and this was used to set the unit at the right height above the deck. The jig was used as a guide when drilling the four leg holes, which were made deep

The model partly assembled. The two 35ft medium-speed boats are on their supporting platform, which sits over the 4in shell hoists at the head of the Simplex chain conveyor. The forward 4in turret has yet to be fitted. Welding gas bottles can be seen in their rack (top left against the side of the house). A temporary fixing screw is protruding from the timber store.

enough to clear the random lengths of the legs. This saved drilling one hole and each raft was then at its correct height, sitting on the hydrostatic valve.

Propellers

What I wanted for this model were proper cast bronze propellers. I could make up propellers myself but these never look quite right as the blade does not flow into the boss, so I had Simon Higgins of Propshop cast me four propellers that were perfect except the boss was the wrong shape. I machined the tail end off the boss and replaced it with a turned bronze pointed exit cone of the correct shape. I lacquered them before attaching them to stainless steel shafts.

The crane

Towards the end of the War most ships had lost their aircraft, leaving air reconnaissance to specialist ships.

Belfast retained her crane, albeit re-sited, to handle her boats. To make a good job of this prominent feature was essential; too many models show cranes built of vastly overscale components. Luckily the 'Anatomy' volume showed three views of the 6/7-ton electric seaplane crane at 1/100th scale. This was more than a great deal of help although I found slight differences between the drawing and what was actually fitted. I reduced the drawings using a Xerox machine to 1/150th scale. The motors, gear boxes, pulleys etc were turned, the rest etched. I actually drew out each length of L or U rolled steel section, numbering each piece for identification on the etching drawing.

Some parts were made of Perspex, such as the resistance boxes. I even machined cooling fins on these with a 0.010in slitting saw. This was largely wasted effort as on the finished model they were not really vis-

ible, but when the whole assembly was painted it looked very impressive standing by itself. When I fitted it to the model I made the mistake of putting the jib in the housed position where it was largely hidden by the two 35ft medium-speed motor boats. It would have looked better with the jib elevated.

4in HA Mk XIX mounting secondary armament

The main problem was the shape of the turret shell. It seemed to me that

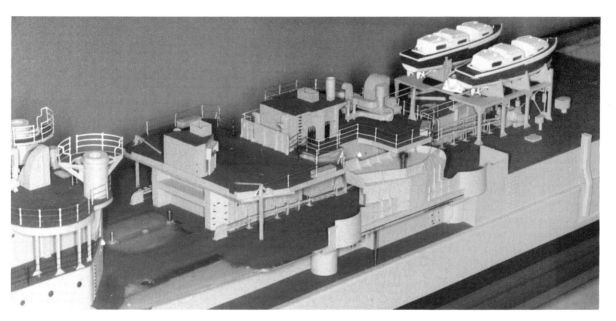

The after end of the Simplex chain conveyor can be seen at the side of the deckhouse. Just forward of this is the RAS (Refuelling At Sea) station. Funnels and other items have yet to be fitted, but their locating pins are in place.

it ought to be possible to develop the shape and form it up. I made a hardwood former and spent hours cutting out paper patterns. When I thought I had it right I cut the pattern from litho plate which enabled me to 'tin bash' the shape around the former; litho plate stays 'put', unlike paper. I finally got it right; cut the shapes from 0.007in brass and soldered up four turret shells. The interiors, fuze setters etc, were just pieces of Perspex. The blast bags were made from Milliput which has the capability of being worked up whilst still wet.

The real difficulty with the secondary armament was making the unique Simplex chain conveyors which carried the ammunition from the hoists situated amidships just forward of the fore funnel to aft of the aft funnel. In the original configuration, when there were three twin turrets each side, they went even further aft. These conveyors were only fitted to *Belfast* and her sistership *Edinburgh*. The trouble was that on *Belfast* they had

been removed, probably when she was used as an accommodation vessel, and only the pads on the deck remained. I had to fall back on the 'Anatomy' volume to make these. I was not sure how accurate my interpretation was but they are not very noticeable on the model itself.

Ventilation fans and ducting

During the last extended refit at Devonport, between January 1956 and May 1959, major changes were made to fit the ship for nuclear warfare. To counter nuclear fallout the ship was fitted with an airtight citadel and a new enclosed bridge. Watertight integrity was improved and pre-wetting facilities installed. This meant that all over the superstructure are fans, motors and ducting; sometimes quite elaborate ducting. These certainly improved the visual interest and were made from Perspex and brass turnings.

There is no doubt that high quality modelmaking requires, amongst other things, the very greatest care in research, particularly with respect to detail. For instance, it is surprising how much can be gleaned from examining the shadows thrown by ob-

jects. However, shadows can also introduce detail that is not there so care is required. It also requires flexibility in techniques and the application of those techniques.

Perhaps the greatest requirement is dedication. This is what carries you through the bad patches, and keeps you going until completion.

Specification *(as completed in 1939)*

Length overall: 613ft 6in
Beam: 63ft 4in
Displacement (during trials): 10,420 tons
Draught: 17ft 3in
Shaft horse power: 80,000 (300rpm)
Speed: 32.5kts
Oil fuel capacity: 2400 tons
Armament: 12-6in in triple turrets
    12-4in HA/LA in twin mountings
    16-2pdr AA in 8-barrelled mountings
    8-0.5in AA in quadruple mountings
    6-21in torpedo tubes in triple mountings
    15 Mk VII depth charges
Aircraft: 2 or 3 Supermarine Walrus amphibians
Armour: Main belt 4½in NC
    Bulkheads 2½in NC
    Decks 3in NC (over magazines), 2in NC (over machinery)

History

Belfast was launched from the shipyard of Harland and Wolff, Belfast, on 17 March 1938. On the 21 November 1939, in the Firth of Forth, a magnetic mine exploded abreast 'A' boiler room breaking her back. She was towed to Rosyth and after great efforts docked down. The damage was so great she was almost scrapped. However, Rosyth made temporary repairs enabling her to reach Devonport where she was straightened out and structurally reinforced. She joined the 10th Cruiser Squadron on 10 December 1942. She then had a hard active career participating in the sinking of the *Scharnhorst* and the action against the *Tirpitz*.

Between August 1944 and April 1945 she was refitted on the Tyne to prepare for action in the Pacific. This refit included an array of close-range AA to counter Kamakaze attacks and to deal with the rigours of a tropical climate.

A short refit was undertaken in Sydney Dockyard in August 1945. In 1948 a further refit was done at Portsmouth. After the Korean War she paid off in November 1952 at Chatham joining Class III Reserve. This looked like the end but in 1955 it was decided to modernise her extensively with the threat of nuclear war hanging in the air. This was done at Portsmouth between 1956 and 1959 before she recommissioned for the Far East. She finally paid off in 1963 into the reserve and was, at one stage, used as an accommodation vessel for maintenance crews on reserve ships.

In 1971 she was saved from the breaker's yard by a trust and is now preserved as a museum ship moored in the Pool of London, where she is open to the public.

Finally, I wish to thank all those who have helped me, especially John Roberts and Ross Watton, for their advice and loan of materials; the staff on *Belfast*, particularly Geoff Ward, for allowing me to go where others cannot; and my friend David Watkin for taking many of the photographs of the model.

References

ROSS WATTON, *The Cruiser Belfast* (Anatomy of the Ship), London 1985

IMPERIAL WAR MUSEUM, *HMS Belfast*

WILLIAM WALLER, *HMS Belfast*, London

JOHN CAMPBELL, *Naval Weapons of World War Two*, London 1985

JOHN BOWEN (ed), *Scale Model Warships*, London 1978

Admiralty DNC Dept drawing No 8/661, four sheets, April 1956
Profile – Sheet 1
Bridge, Superstructure & forecastle deck – Sheet 2
No 2 (Upper) & No 3 (Lower) decks – Sheet 3
No 4 (Platform) & No 5 (Hold) decks – Sheet 4

The completed model. Note the mirror at the after end of the baseboard to allow propeller and shaft details to be seen.

Photographs by the author and David Watkin.

Confederacy

Continental Frigate – 1778

by Justin Camarata

The building of this model came about pretty much by chance – or was it fate? About seven years ago, as I was browsing in a local art gallery that dealt in ship models, I noticed a man closely examining a model of the brig *Lexington* made by a friend of mine, Jim Creighton. In conversation with this man I found that he was English, was working in the States for the next few years, and was interested in commissioning a model of a vessel of Revolutionary War period.

He was particularly taken with *Lexington*'s rigging and asked if I thought Jim would build something for him. He also specified, however, that the hull had to be plank-on-frame construction rather than solid like that of the *Lexington*. Knowing Jim was not keen on plank-on-frame work, I took a deep breath and made the rash proposal that I do the hull and Jim provide the rig. Carrying out such a proposal would be a significant stretch for me for though I had built a number of models professionally this would be the first plank-on-frame effort.

Somewhat to my surprise, but to my great delight, the commission went forward. After much discussion the frigate *Confederacy* was selected as the subject. Jim was to do the masts, yards, rigging, boats and cannon and I was to do the rest. Jim began to make parts and I dug into the hull. For various reasons my end of the work moved along rather slowly. For

Starboard side of the completed model.

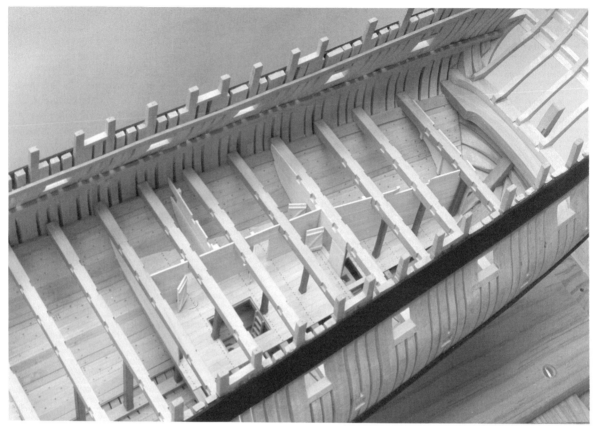

After platforms with bulkheads for captain's and lieutenant's store rooms.

one, much unforeseen research had to be done regarding the framing disposition. In addition, the client, having commissioned several models previously, was well aware of the tedious nature of much of the work, and anxious that I do my best he urged me to interrupt his project whenever I felt my enthusiasm flagging. This I did, I must confess, with some regularity.

It was almost five years before the model was ready for the rig. Unfortunately, by that time Jim was unable to carry on and it fell to me to finish the model. At times the long-term nature of the project made it seem never-ending. This feeling was strongest about halfway through the hull after I had put a good many more hours into it than expected and was becoming acutely aware of the significant amount of work yet to be done. It was

also somewhat distressing to look at work in the model that had been done a few years back and realise that if redone it probably would be improved. Finally, I must admit that when the model was delivered it left one mighty big hole in the shop. It's difficult not to form an emotional attachment to a project that has been an integral part of your life for so long.

The ship

Confederacy was chosen as the subject for three reasons. The client wanted a Continental frigate; good source material was available on the ship and, being longer for her beam than most contemporary frigates, she had a certain unique aesthetic appeal.

Confederacy's service record is not exactly what you would call sparkling; she never fired a shot in anger. Launched in November 1778, she made only two major and relatively

short voyages before being captured in April 1781. Her first mission was to sail for France with the French Minister and the American Minister to Spain aboard. This task was aborted twelve days out by a severe storm which damaged the rig and rudder. *Confederacy* limped into Martinique where she remained for some time.

On her second voyage, an out and back trip to Haiti for military supplies, she was intercepted by HMS *Roebuck* and the frigate HMS *Orpheus*. Outgunned, the decision was made to surrender the ship. She was taken to New York, surveyed and subsequently brought into the Royal Navy as *Confederate*. A few months later she was declared unfit for service and disappeared from the records. As she was probably built from green timbers her demise was very likely caused by overwhelming rot damage. *Confederacy*'s builders did not have large stocks of seasoned wood on hand nor, due to the on-going war, did they have the time to let the ship sit in frame and harden up. The entire project, short of the rig and fitting out, was completed in a little over a year and a half.

While her exploits and lifespan may have left something to be desired, her design was definitely noteworthy. The fact that a survey was done and draughts made of her lines and structure is a partial testament to the interest in her at the time. *Confederacy*'s hull shape was experimental. As Howard I Chapelle put it in *The History of the American Sailing Navy*, she was 'almost a galley-frigate' bringing to mind a rather fine-hulled vessel. Compared to most contemporary frigates *Confederacy* was indeed longer overall, smaller in beam and shallower in draft. Such departures did permit a sharper entry and longer run, features which should have improved speed and perhaps weatherliness.

The term galley-frigate also seemed appropriate to Chapelle in light of the small ports on the berth deck which could have been for sweeps. Certain British frigates of the period did apparently employ sweeps but it baffles me to think how long sweeps could effectively be shipped and unshipped in a vessel as crowded below as was *Confederacy*. Perhaps these ports were merely for much needed ventilation.

Confederacy was one of the close forerunners of the well known 44-gun American frigates such as the *Constitution* and *Constellation*. Less than twenty years elapsed between *Confederacy*'s launch and that of her later sisters. That certain aspects of design and construction were carried forward and improved in the later class was not due just to time proximity. There is evidence that the designer Joshua Humphreys was intimately involved in the conception of all of these vessels. As will be further discussed below, this connection became very important to me as research progressed.

On a more personal note, *Confed-*

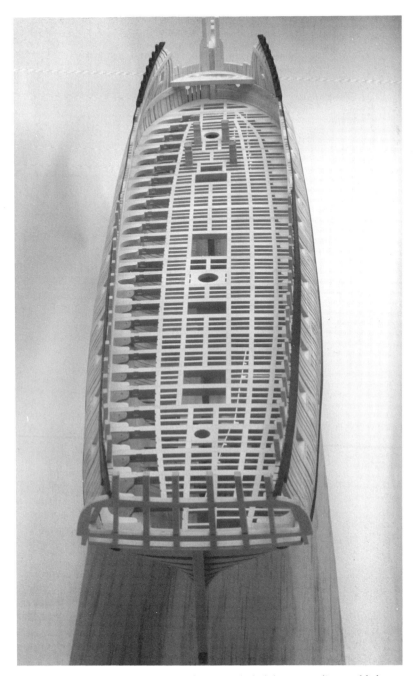

Berth deck beams, carlines and ledges.

eracy's keel was laid in Norwich, Connecticut, which is only about twenty miles from my shop. Norwich stands at the head of the Thames River some ten miles from Long Island Sound. Today it is very difficult to envisage her being built there for nothing in sight resembles a shipyard. Local records indicate, however, that shipbuilding was a definite presence in Norwich in the late 1700s, but further hint that the *Confederacy* project was extraordinary in scope. It must have been quite an event when she was launched and subsequently towed down river to New London to be rigged.

The research

Prime source materials were the aforementioned Admiralty Survey and the associated draughts. Dr D H Robinson's article *The Continental Frigate Confederacy* published in the *Nautical Research Journal* (Vol 8, No 2, March-April, 1956) reprinted the survey and provided some historical background. In *The History of the American Sailing Navy* Howard Chapelle presented his version of the draughts along with a spar and sail plan based on Admiralty recordings.

Fortunately, from my point of view, William Crothers of Seagull Plans had carefully reviewed all this material along with that from several other sources including the journal of Joseph Hardy, captain of marines aboard *Confederacy*. He was also given Dr Robinson's original files from which his article was written. Crothers draughted a very complete and beautifully executed set of drawings of the hull and rig. It is basically from these drawings that the model was built.

Dr Robinson's files included spar dimensions as recorded by Joshua Humphreys in one of his notebooks archived by the Historical Society of Pennsylvania. Crothers recreated his spar plan based on these dimensions and hence the rig on the model is, as best we can tell, as it was at the time of launch. Rig configuration did change significantly over the short life of the ship. In addition to the storm damage already mentioned, which required considerable re-rigging, the mainmast was sprung on the way to Haiti and there is evidence the rig was cut down after capture.

Crothers' plans were missing one vital piece of information. The client had specified that framing was not to be done in Admiralty style, rather it was to follow as closely as possible to that in the original vessel. Since the Admiralty Survey only provided a few molded and sided dimensions for

The completed berth deck.

futtocks and top timbers Crothers elected to leave this part of the model to the builder's discretion.

Coming up with a convincing, or at least arguable, framing disposition took a bit of doing. Not a whole lot of hard evidence is available relative to Continental shipbuilding practices. Reconstructing the disposition settled upon required input from contemporary English and French naval framing practices, underwater archaeology studies, somewhat later but known framing of American Naval vessels, and common sense structural considerations, among others.

A detailed discussion of the arguments for the disposition used was presented in a *Seaways* magazine article (Vol 2, No 1, January/February, 1991). Briefly summarising, the rationale was as follows. Joshua Humphreys and the builders in Norwich were probably strongly influenced by their British cousins. On the other hand, Continental builders were known to be innovative and open to experiment. It might therefore be expected that *Confederacy*'s framing would bear some resemblance to that of a British frigate but that it might also incorporate some significant differences.

A major clue to a possible difference was furnished by the still existing frigate USS *Constitution*. In 1876 she underwent an extensive restoration in which most of the topside planking was removed. Photographs of her in this condition showed the framing quite clearly. Bounding each side of a gunport was a double thickness frame or bend as per a typical British frigate of the period. Between these bends and in the way of the gunport were two single thickness frames or fillers. This arrangement also followed British practice. However, between the gunports there were typically three filler frames rather than the two of *Constitution*'s British counterparts. Recalling Joshua

Gun deck, showing beams, carlines and ledges.

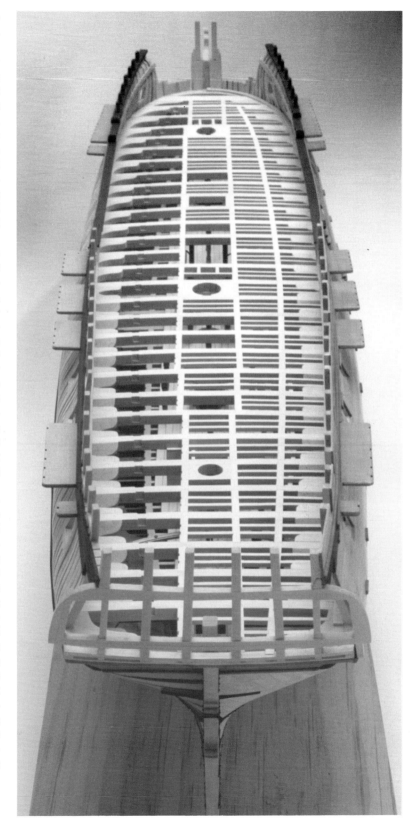

Humphrey's design involvement in *Constitution* and *Confederacy* it seemed acceptable to apply this departure in construction to *Confederacy*'s framing. It became apparent that a very logical and structurally sound disposition would result if four filler frames were inserted between each gunport with the centre two in each group bounding the sweep or vent ports (Figure 1).

Considering the 'stretched' nature of the hull relative to most frigates, it seems reasonable to accept the extra fillers as a means of lengthening the ship. There are a few variations in this pattern. As in British vessels, there is a group of three fillers near the centre of the ship. It is at this location that the floors probably shifted sides on the bends. Two other groups of three fillers exist near the

Beams in place for the foredeck, boat skids and quarter deck.

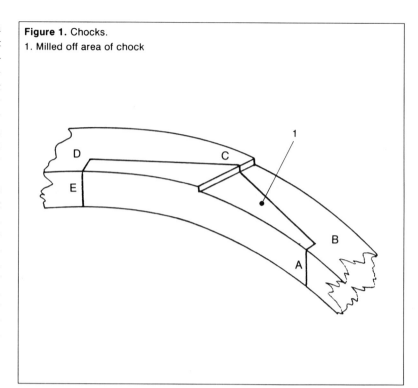

Figure 1. Chocks.
1. Milled off area of chock

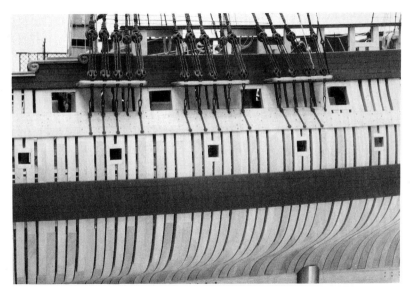

notes that *Confederacy*'s deck beams were supported by one dagger knee on each side of the vessel. No mention is made of hanging knees. *Constitution*'s kneeing arrangement generally consists of two dagger knees and a hanging knee. Dagger knees could have been an early attempt to introduce more torsional or twisting stiffness into the hull (akin to the later Seppings system of diagonal bracing). Considering that *Constitution* was the heavier built vessel by far, adding the extra dagger knees would seem to be a logical extension of the design philosophy exhibited in *Confederacy*.

The model

Disposition of midship frames—note the four filler frames between the gunports.

Port after quarterdeck. Port half of upper decks left unplanked for viewing below.

ends for which I have no good argument. Perhaps it was just a way of making the overall length come out right.

Another structural link connects the two ships. The Admiralty Survey

A scale of $^3/_{16}$in to the foot was used to build the model. Rather than describe the construction in complete detail let me touch on a few areas which might be of special interest.

One of these areas is the framing.

Foredeck. The gratings over the stove are of etched brass.

Midships, with berth deck and platform visible through the main hatch.

To construct the framing with bends and fillers having all the appropriate components (including chocks), properly shaped in the molded direction, and stepped down in the sided dimension from keel to cap rail was daunting, particularly since I hadn't done it before. Unfortunately, I came up with no clever, quick way of meeting these requirements that was satisfactory to me and so I was faced with building up each frame individually. Undoubtedly, many ingenious model builders could improve on my tedious 'brute force' procedures. I describe them in the hope that some aspects of what I did may be found useful.

The outboard shape of each frame was determined using a fairly simple programme written for my personal computer. Offsets from station positions on the lines drawing were fed into the programme. What came out was a table of offsets for each frame at its fore and aft station on the keel. These dimensions were plotted and the inside contours laid out using a

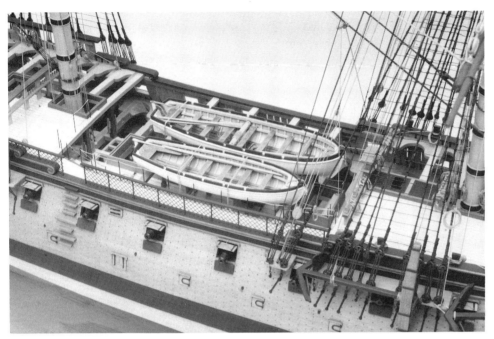

Deck amidships, showing barge and cutter. Deck and bottom planking of holly; topsides, pillars and coamings pear; remainder boxwood; netting etched brass.

Galleries. Windows glazed with 0.005in glass sheet mounted behind etched brass frames.

Starboard quarter. Yards, cap rail and wales painted with a 70/30 mixture of flat black and flat white paints.

systematically changing molded dimension from keel to cap. Locations of floors, futtocks and top timbers were noted on the plots. The programme was set up to treat cant as well as full frames. Armed with these drawings as templates the various components could be accurately made.

Before proceeding further, perhaps a few words on chocks are in order. Chocks do add measurably to the strength of a frame, particularly for a filler (see Figure 1). In fact, I do not see how a proper filler can be done without them. Following David White's drawings of the frigate *Diana* in the Anatomy of the Ship series,

chocks should be about four times the local frame molded dimension in length and about two-thirds the local frame molded dimension in width at their widest point. While shown shorter in some other sources a longer chock clearly means a stronger joint. Chocks in frames having a significant bevel might well be reduced in width so that they are not cut into from the outside when fairing up the hull exterior.

First let me describe how a single thickness filler frame was constructed. Floors, futtocks and top timbers were rough cut from properly sided stock using paper patterns glued to the stock with rubber cement. About $1/16$in of extra stock was allowed all around except for the ends where components would be joined to each other.

These surfaces were cut precisely.

The drawing of the frame was taped to a flat surface with a piece of waxed paper taped over it. The keel slot in the floor was cut, or, if the frame had first futtocks, they were joined and the keel slot milled in the assembly. Components of the frame were butt-glued to each other over the template drawing. Chock locations were drawn in on the pattern paper glued to the frame components. A razor blade was used to cut along these lines and the paper where the chock was to be was removed. Doing so made the area to be cut away much easier to see.

After removing the frame from the assembly board a fine, narrow-bladed band saw was used to rough cut the chock opening. From this point until the chocks were in place care had to be taken not to unduly stress the butt joints. The frame was then clamped to the bed plate of a milling machine with a thin sheet of disposable stock between the frame and bed plate. A $1/_{16}$in diameter end mill was inserted in the chuck. Cuts AB and DE in Figure 1 were made followed by cuts BC and CD. To align the frame for the last two cuts the bed plate was rotated without unclamping the frame. A straight-edge was placed along the edge of the chock opening and the bed plate rotated until the straight-edge was parallel to the traverse bed longitudinal axis. Corners B and D were cleaned up with a sharp knife.

Chock shapes were traced on stock of proper thickness using the cut opening as a pattern. The frame was remounted over the assembly board and held in place with dressmaker's pins. Chocks were final fitted by dressing with a disc sander and glued in place.

When removed from the assembly board all was surprisingly strong. At this point the frame was faired to the contours of the paper patterns (allowing some material for final fairing in place) and the paper removed. The last step was to mill off a portion of the side of the chock as shown in Figure 1 so that the sided step from futtock to futtock was repeated in the chock.

A bend was built in essentially the same manner. Two halves were made separately and glued back to back before fairing of the outside contours. Care had to be taken that the basic frame drawing was symmetrical and that the keel slot and top timbers were accurately aligned when gluing together.

With all this fancy frame construction and associated research put into the model there was much discussion with the client as to how best to display it. Since the interior was to be fully detailed we talked also about how much of the below decks area was to be visible. The decision was

Main top.

made to leave the port side unplanked except in the way of the backing links. All the frames were to be included rather than omitting some for internal viewing purposes. Both of us felt that unnatural holes in the side of the vessel seriously disturbed the continuity of line.

In order to see into the interior it was decided to plank only about half of each deck. This approach was more successful than I thought it might be. There are, however, many details below which can no longer be seen by normal means (ie, without fibre optics or x-rays). An extensive series of photographs was taken so a record exists. The manner in which the model is displayed is quite helpful in making it easy to see what can be seen. It is in a glass case mounted somewhat lower than usual so looking down on the deck is not difficult. In its normal position the case forms an integral part of a large section of a wall cabinet. Three sides of the model are visible. The most unusual feature of the cabinet is that the display case portion of it slides away from the wall on very sturdy tracks. In this position the model and case can be rotated on a built-in turntable through 360 degrees, allowing the model to be viewed from any angle.

The carvings

The manner in which the carvings were done was also a bit unusual. On a past commission the client had engaged Steve Morrison, an artist in England, to do the carvings and wished to do so again. I made the wood pieces on which the carvings were to go, such as the taffarel, head timbers and bow rails. A dummy stem was made for the figurehead and a contoured block, matched to the hull cross section just forward of the galleries, was provided for the decorative flourishes fastened to the planking at that location.

These pieces, along with full-sized drawings, were sent along to Morrison. He fashioned the decorations from Milliput, a two-part epoxy. Those decorations not applied directly to the wood model components provided were done on a paper backing. All of the unmounted carvings were flat except for the piece on the contoured block. All of the paper-backed work was done over wire

frames applied to the paper.

Having to have these carvings prepared well before I needed them made me a little nervous about the way they would fit when the time came to install them. In the event most of the parts were fine, but I did have a little difficulty with two foremost head timbers supporting the rails. In order to achieve a good fit most of the carving had to be ground away. Following Morrison's lead I re-did the removed scrollwork with Milliput. The material went on very nicely. One major advantage it has is that it will set underwater. At first that may not seem like such a big thing but this characteristic does permit much freedom in smoothing and otherwise working the material using a water moistened tool.

The carvings were painted prior to installation. It is quite likely the originals were also painted (rather than gilded). Since the colour is unknown a brownish golden yellow was chosen for all but the figurehead to complement the box, pear and holly woods in the model.

A number of brass etched parts were used. These included port lid hinges, backing links, gallery window frames and letters for the ship's name on the stern. Window frames were glazed with 0.005in thick laboratory slide glass. The name letters were painted and then pinned to the model using 0.010in diameter brass wire.

The rig

Finally, a few words on the rig. All of the blocks are solid box with about half of them having turned brass sheaves. With the exception of the lightest of lines, all of the rope used

Starboard quarter view of the completed model.

Photographs by the author

was spun up on a ropewalk, taking due notice of what was supposed to be cable – and what was hawser-laid. White cotton-covered polyester thread was used for the spinning stock. The standing rigging was coloured using a blend of shoe dyes formulated specifically for cloth shoes. The colour is not black but a very dark brown. Ground earth pigments suspended in a mixture of turpentine and beeswax were used to tint the running rigging a light tan.

In the autumn of 1993 the model retraced the original ship's path across the Atlantic aboard the *Queen Elizabeth II*, passed docilely through a force 10 storm, and reached its final destination shortly thereafter. ❑